RECORDAR ES VÍVIR

TO REMEMBER IS TO LIVE

SFERNANDO CARMONA

CARMONA
PUBLISHING

Recordar es Vivir

© 2025 **SFernando Carmona**

Published by **Carmona Publishing**

Printed in the United States of America

ISBN: 979-8-9937793-1-7

Cover design by Carmona Publishing

Interior design by Carmona Publishing

First Edition — 2025

 Formatted with Vellum

Dedication

To my daughters Eunice, Dennice and Jannice

May your hearts always remember where love began, and may you carry our story wherever life leads you.

INTRODUCTION

Every memory is a sigh of the soul, an echo returning from time itself to remind us who we are and where we come from. This book is born from the heart, from the desire to rescue small fragments of life that remained floating among the memories of my homeland, the beloved faces of my friends, the places that marked my life, and the moments that, although distant now, still beat within me even when time and distance try to erase them.

Here intertwine the days of childhood under the blazing sun, the games played on dusty streets, the smell of freshly baked bread from the kitchen, and the dear voices that still resonate in my memory. Each story is an open window to a past that refuses to disappear, a tribute to those who walked beside me and left footprints that forgetfulness has never been able to erase.

I remember my homeland as one remembers an eternal love, with tenderness, with gratitude, and with a nostalgia that sometimes hurts, yet also comforts. My homeland is not just a place on a map, it is an emotion that lives in the soul, a song carried in the blood. Its green mountains, its burning sun, its salty breeze, and its endless sea are witnesses to stories that deserve to be told.

Family has always been the refuge where everything begins and where one always returns. Friends are the brothers that life gave me beyond my home, companions in joyful days and witnesses to difficult times. With them I shared dreams, songs, and silences, learning that true friendship is measured not by years, but by the mark it leaves upon the heart.

The sea has always been my confidant. In its rhythm I learned to listen to the murmur of life. Its vastness reminds me that, although time may change the shores, the waves always return. So too do memories return, sometimes as gentle as foam and other times as deep as the horizon. The sea keeps within its song the voice of my land and the echo of all those who once departed but never truly left.

Writing these pages is a return home. I have felt the

embrace of my people, the murmur of the sea, the music of the *cuatro*, and the taste of the simple life that shaped us. It is a journey into the past, but also an act of love toward the present. In every word there is love, there is gratitude, and there is also a sweet melancholy for what was and is no more yet remains alive in the heart. It is my way of giving thanks, of honoring, and of keeping alive the essence of those who taught me that roots, when tended with love, can bloom anywhere.

Because to remember is more than to recall the past, it is to relive it, to honor it, to keep the flame alive that ties us to our roots. To remember is to live again, to feel once more the warmth of an embrace, the sound of laughter, the scent of the sea upon the skin. To remember is to affirm that we are still alive, that we still exist, despite time, distance, or forgetfulness, as children of a land that taught us to dream with the heart. May these memories serve as a song of love to Puerto Rico, to family, and to friendship, to all that, in remembering it, makes us live once again.

PROLOGUE

BY; PROFESSOR KELVIN FUENTES ROSAS, M.A.
EDUCATIONAL LEADERSHIP

I n times when the culture and values of nations are constantly threatened by an ever-growing global influx, there are few spaces left where singularity can reveal the beauty of its heritage and make itself visible to those who delight in its riches. Thus, we become witnesses to the diversity that marks a milestone in the history of the world's peoples and cultures. Art, in all its expressions, is enriched by this cultural influence, one that goes beyond the instruments that drive the commercialization of culture, elevating it instead to a cognitive and educational plane.

History, therefore, echoes unique cultural imaginaries, as is the case of Puerto Rico, an imagination that can be expressed in such ingenious ways that it awakens feelings of cultural patriotism and serves as a guide for those far from their native land. This singular function of narrative has the power to turn our senses into a sea of emotions, evoking the very nature of what it means to be Puerto Rican. It goes beyond the mere fact of having been born here; it is about *feeling* that one belongs here, even when far from the homeland that saw us born.

In this book, written in an impressively reflective historical tone, we are led by the hand to experience the senses of a Puerto Rican who, through memory, takes us down the corridors of a not-so-distant past, one marked by exile and return. That exile whose effects so many of us feel, and that return which represents the triumph of those who leave, longing to come back. In the end, what will always matter are the memories of the good days, the bad ones, and the better ones. Through this journey we perceive the spirit of a man who lived, thought, spoke, and acted as a *puertorro* of his time, one who gathered the best of the island's northwest and sprinkles it throughout his work with the mischievous, unmistakable language of a true *borincano*. From the sea, the countryside, and the town to the *carro público,* the airplane, and the climb up and down the hills, this book offers us a living fragment of our island.

When the book delves into our politics, philosophy, and religions, it does so as one who paints brushstrokes on a sketchbook filled with colors that make it unique. For our homeland's ideals carry essences that are masterfully presented in this work. With casual subtlety, our author portrays love and family as a tender comedy set in some corner of our island, without a doubt, an ode to the commitment to the dreams of home and country.

Turning our illusions into reality through reading and making each letter echo deep within our Puerto Rican being, is the path that leads us to affirm that you hold in your hands an excellent literary work, one that will allow a greater understanding of our Puerto Rican idiosyncrasy. Without question, it is a valuable instrument that will help future generations understand better who we are and where we are headed.

CHAPTER I

WHEN HOMELAND CALLS YOUR NAME

After so many years away from the place that shaped him, life now moved too quickly for him to catch his breath, much less look back and say goodbye. His little island had waited for him longer than he ever expected, and now it was calling him home with a quiet urgency he could no longer ignore. One last gathering with a few old friends let him walk the familiar corners he had carried in his heart. And the goodbyes with his family had stretched into tender, heavy weeks, each farewell a reminder of how much he had left behind.

It was a cold morning when he said farewell to the home that had sheltered him for the past forty years. Snow had fallen the night before, and the day glowed with that pale, wintry light that only a winter sun can offer. Ironically, it was the perfect day to stay indoors.

His feelings were a quiet storm of happiness, sadness, and fear. He walked through the house one last time, room by room, and the memories rose around him like scenes from an old film. His wife, his children, every pet, the celebrations, the joys, the sorrows, all of it burst forth like a shimmering mix of beautiful recollections he wished he could carry with him.

Every corner held a story. As he ran his hand along the walls, he could almost hear his daughters' laughter bouncing down the hallway. He remembered the births of his grandchildren as if those days had never truly passed. And when he stepped into the kitchen, he could see the gentle ghost of his wife, smiling as she kneaded, crushed, and ground ingredients for a dish everyone loved. It felt as if he were walking through the living heart of their shared life.

He had grown so attached to the house that he no longer saw it as a structure, but as a quiet companion who had listened to every joy and every sorrow without ever asking for anything in return. This home had been his comfort, his refuge. He knew every crack in the floor and every scratch on the walls. He loved it for its imperfections. Each mark held a piece of his family's story.

It had been his sanctuary. Here, relatives and

friends gathered on Christmas, on Thanksgiving Day, on Easter Sunday, on birthdays, and on days when no celebration was needed except being together. Within these walls, the physical wounds of his daughters had been tended, and the emotional wounds of many children who came into his life had been gently held and healed.

He stepped outside to take one last look from a distance. Emotions were never easy for him, yet in that moment he felt them all rising at once. His eyes filled with tears, and the cold air froze them lightly as they slid down his cheeks. The morning chill bit into him, but the deeper ache came from the nostalgia already settling into his bones. The house stood quietly behind him, almost as if it were breathing with him, offering a final, silent farewell.

Then a single tear slipped free, soft and unguarded, and with it the strength he had been trying to hold on to, gave way. He was not crying only for the walls he was leaving behind, but for the years lived inside them, for the tiredness he had carried, for the memories that refused to be packed away, for the losses he had never dared to speak aloud. The mix of happiness, sadness, and fear rose gently but powerfully, wrapping around him as he let go of the place that had shaped him more deeply than he had ever admitted.

He had grown vulnerable to his own emotions. The last few years had been the hardest. He cried every time he heard La Borinqueña, and the thought of leaving forever made him sentimental in ways he could not explain. This place had formed him, broken him, and rebuilt him. More than once, he had needed to hit bottom to find the strength to rise again.

The instability, the politics, the crime, the rising cost of living, all of it had become a weight he could no longer carry. It felt as if only yesterday a shy, uncertain young man had boarded an Eastern Airlines plane toward an unknown life, and now he was returning home because he felt he had lost his purpose, moving through life as if on autopilot, slowly fading inside.

„„AND HE TOOK OFF

The last days and nights blurred together in a bittersweet haze, heavy with the pressure of leaving. Life away from his homeland had been shaky at first, but in the end, it had given him more than he ever expected, and he knew he would miss much of it. He had grown fond of the four seasons of snowflakes drifting quietly, of spring flowers opening like small miracles, of summer storms, of autumn's firelit colors. He had learned to move with the rhythm of crowded sidewalks and busy city streets. His feelings tangled inside him. Maybe he needed to be braver, but his heart kept whispering that it was time to go home. When the day of departure arrived, he rose early for the airport. He was a naturally joyful man, but that morning sadness and anxiety settled over him with surprising weight.

The airport was a gigantic steel cocoon, and people moved in and out of its doors like small wasps, each with a different destination. The beams held up countless windows that let in so much light you could almost fool yourself into thinking it was a summer day. Voices of young people, elderly people, and children echoed through the space. Some gathered in a corner to cry in anticipation of separation. Others showed excitement because they were leaving on vacation.

He moved with shaky steps toward the customer service counter, but he knew he had to keep going, leaving behind an entire lifetime of memories. He walked toward the plane wrapped in a breeze of uncertainty. He was not sure what awaited him on the other side, but he felt that every step he took toward the gate was a promise, the promise to keep growing and to take with him everything he loved. In the distance he heard Christmas music playing, and a small smile formed on his lips.

As he boarded the plane he could not stop looking back, as if he had forgotten something. When the plane pulled away from the gate an avalanche of memories rushed through his mind, and he tried to hold on to them. It was too hard in that moment.

The plane took off and his heart began to race. As the aircraft climbed, he felt the ground slipping away, and with it, a very important part of his life. In his chest, sadness blended with a calm stillness. Up there, time seemed to stop. Between the clouds and the sky, he lost himself in his thoughts. It was a strange sensation, to be nowhere and everywhere at the same time. Through the small airplane window, he could see the snow on the rooftops of the houses. The city looked cold. He had flown on these planes so many times. He could curl up and fall asleep as easily as when he dozed off on the couch. The hum of the engines was like a lullaby. The plane felt like a pause between two worlds, the one that had shaped him and the one waiting ahead. Every mile he traveled away from his home stretched a thread between what had been and what would be. This would be his heavenly cradle for the next few hours, rocked by the winds, between cotton clouds and far above the sea.

As soon as the plane reached a comfortable altitude, he was interrupted so they could serve lunch. Airplane food arrived wrapped in small plastic containers, warm and without much smell, so different from the dishes back home. Everything was in its place, measured and packaged, but nothing tasted the same. While he tasted it, he could not stop thinking of the food from his house, of the smell of sofrito filling the kitchen. You can say whatever you want about airplane meals, but it is a meal you always look forward to. You are flying at thirty thousand feet and still blessed with the fruits of the earth. In those long hours sitting there, you must eat something. So, he criticized it, smiled, ate it, and kept eating.

With his eyes on the horizon full of clouds of every size and shape, he thought about his achievements and how much he had changed and grown. The aerial view invited new ideas and turned him into a philosopher. He was no longer the young boy who had arrived here full of illusions and dreams. He carried with him an emotional suitcase filled with memories of people and the things he had accomplished and would never forget. The truth was that he had grown old in another place. He felt sad and preferred to fall asleep to avoid thinking.

As the plane descended, he looked down at the spectacular immensity of the landscape filled with mountains and beaches along the coast of his home-land, and he was left breathless. It was the moment when the heart beats stronger, when memories and reality merge with the shine of the sea and the colors of the land. That deep blue of the ocean that resembles no other. The coastline gleaming, alive, as if the sun had chosen it for itself. The colorful houses, the mountains dressed in green. And, years later, those same rooftops covered in blue tarps, silent witnesses of María's passing. The emotion rose from his chest to his eyes, a mix of joy, nostalgia, and home. His homeland looked small but felt immense in his soul. It was as if his heart, too, descended toward the ground where he had learned to love and dream.

The plane touched down, and for a second everything fell silent. Then, like a wave crashing on the shore, the passengers erupted into an enthusiastic applause. It was a magical moment, so distinctly theirs, so full of emotion and pride. It was an impulse shared from the soul. That applause was more than a custom, it was an expression of the Puerto Rican spirit, a mix of relief and gratitude for letting them return to their land once more.

As soon as he picked up his luggage, the heat hit him like a slap. He smiled when he realized the heat and humidity were here to stay and would never disappear. In his homeland there were only hot days, rainy days, and days when it simply did not rain. He paused for a moment, hesitating, as if sinking into the new reality that offered no choice but to move forward and understand what it meant to start over.

He felt strange, and he could not explain why.

Everything seemed the same, yet different. There was an invisible disorganization in the air, a familiar chaos that now felt almost foreign. Without realizing it, he was experiencing the beginning of reverse culture shock.

He heard voices in the distance, quick and melodic, with that accent he had missed so much, and his heart leaped. He felt excited to find a world completely different from his daily routine. He watched people speak with their hands, with their entire bodies, and understood that yes, he had arrived home.

Even so, he felt overwhelmed. The Spanglish flew boldly through the airport halls, so strong and so natural that it almost intimidated him. His emotions collided with each other, until he walked a little farther.

Then his nose recognized something before his mind did, the smell of freshly fried **alcapurrias** coming from a small cart near the terminal corner. That smell was the real stamp of entry into Puerto Rican soil. He ordered an alcapurria and a Cola Champagne. The woman who served him offered a smile so warm it awakened his senses. In that moment he felt his feet truly settle after landing. But something still did not fit.

Had he changed? Or had the island changed?

He was eager to embrace his old friends, catch up with family, and taste his favorite foods. But he also felt butterflies in his stomach, and a restlessness that kept him from breathing fully.

What if he no longer belonged here? What if he no longer knew how to fit back into his own home?

His brother-in-law came to pick him up at the airport. On the way, the island began to reveal itself in small portraits, an old housing project still standing, an elderly woman on her balcony rocking memories, a homeless man sleeping under the warm shade of a tree, boys playing baseball in an abandoned lot, another man lying on a piece of cardboard, an addict asking for coins under a traffic light, and beyond that, new shopping centers shining like recent promises.

They entered the highway. They no longer traveled along the old Number 2 road, but on an expressway called José de Diego. A strange emotion washed over him, so many things had changed. The music blasting from the other cars was different, no longer just salsa or merengue. Now the booming bass thundered so loudly it felt like his eardrums would burst.

He felt a little scared and at the same time excited. He had dreamed of this moment so many times, but now he already missed the soft hands of his grandchildren and their voices calling him, Grandpa.

This return home was stirring everything inside him. He was not only thinking about what was different, but also about what he had lost over the years without even noticing. He fell asleep in the seat, and in his dreams, he understood something his heart had known all along.

Coming home is not arriving at a place. It is the soul recognizing where it belongs.

16

CHAPTER 3
THE BEGINNING OF US

The first time he saw her, the gentle sway of her hips and Marusha's smile captured him entirely. His heart surrendered almost at once, a love so deep it felt as if it had begun long before they ever met.

The first time he tried to kiss her, his heart was pounding, and his lips were almost there when little Monín stopped them, a tiny spy disguised as an angel, the chaperone sent by the god of the house, the father-in-law. They both froze, as if a scratched record had suddenly cut the moment short, and after a flicker of disappointment they simply laughed. "Cold again." In those days, the truest sign of love was the nervous sweat in their hands.

Ah, but the first time he kissed her he closed his

eyes and trembled with fear. Her lips were perfect, pink, soft and full, and he doubted his own could ever match them. To him, she was flawless. But the moment their lips met, a rush of something indescribably tender swept through him, filling his whole body with love and joy. No one else could have given him that feeling. It was as if he were dreaming, and time had quietly stopped. Her lips tasted sweet; her skin felt soft as a cloud. Butterflies rose in his stomach, and when the kiss ended, he felt as if he had conquered the world.

"Did you like it?" he asked, still trembling.

"What do you think?" she answered, offering her lips for a second kiss. In that instant he knew, without doubt, that she was the one.

Love is something difficult to explain. One moment you may be invaded by loneliness, but as soon as you fall in love you feel above the world. There is magic in courtship. You want to feel alive, and maybe a little crazy. You want to kiss in the rain. You want to dance and feel her breath. You want to sing her love songs. When two people are in love the relationship grows quickly and constantly. They say the person you love should make you laugh, but even better is making her laugh. The best moments are those spent holding hands and talking about anything at all.

It was not in a restaurant or at an elegant party, it

was on a bench in a park where he asked her to marry him. It was one of those sunsets that paint the sky orange and pink. The air smelled of flowers, and the breeze played with her hair. He was nervous, with his heart beating like a plena drum. He took the ring out of his pocket, and it felt as if it weighed tons. They had walked for a while, talking about everything and nothing, and when they sat on that bench, he felt the world stop. He took her hand, and without hesitation said, "Will you marry me?" He had no prepared speech, no fancy words from a novel. It was simple, but true. She looked at him, and with that disarming smile, said yes. Right there, on that park bench, their life together began. Marusha would change his life with a heart full of love.

They were married in the town church, and their wedding night was wrapped in a deep, quiet love. What mattered most was that they had chosen to walk through life side by side. In that humble bed, the dreams that would one day become their reality began to take shape. Now united as husband and wife, words felt unnecessary. Perhaps still a little afraid of the fragile new bond between them, they remained in silence, a silence broken only by the steady beat of their hearts. The minister's words lingered in the air, "until death do you part."

In that first nest of love, their kisses were at first sweet and shy, then urgent and passionate, the kind given as if the world were about to end. Curled up together for the first time, they loved each other without hurry, until sleep overtook them. He watched her sleep, and he too drifted off, waiting for the first sunrise at her side.

When he woke up, he felt as though he had grown. There, lying next to her, as he traced her figure softly and stroked her hair, he thought, "Now, yes... now I am a man." She opened her eyes, and he greeted her with a kiss and the announcement that, on top of everything, he was hungry.

It was the first morning in the house that would become their home and little palace. How wonderful it felt to wake to the smell of freshly brewed coffee and almond cookies. Loving as always, she had risen early, excited for her first morning as a wife, and promised to make a warm bowl of oatmeal for breakfast. He watched her from the table with pride as she stirred the pot with such seriousness, as if she were preparing a feast fit for royalty. But when she finally served the plates, the oatmeal was hard, like small stones floating in milk. When he dipped the spoon in, it almost bounced. Still, he looked into her eyes, saw the tenderness with which she had made it, and ate every bite without a word. Because what mattered was not the taste or the texture, but the love that had gone into that breakfast.

"Is something wrong, darling?"

"No, nothing my love. I was just thinking you are the most beautiful woman in the world, and that of all men I am the luckiest one."

She was not foolish. She came closer when she saw him struggling with the spoon, and she began to laugh, and he laughed too. And there, between laughter and difficult bites, they understood that along their journey together there would be things that would not turn out perfect, but that with love everything could be carried more lightly.

Why complain? Not after that night of romance. Not after looking into her tender eyes and seeing the love with which she had prepared that breakfast. He loved her so much he would have been willing to eat that same oatmeal for the rest of his life, but for now all he could do was wait to see how dinner would turn out.

CHAPTER 4
THE MOST LOYAL

L ife is good, of course it is. Waking up next to a beautiful woman, opening the windows wide, and breathing the pure air of his homeland.

How deeply he loved that little piece of Puerto Rican soil. Arecibo, La Villa del Capitán Correa, the Diamond of the North, a joyful, sun-filled town, full of colonial buildings adorned with flowers and bright balconies. Everywhere you went there was a friend from now and a friend from the past. Happy children playing at writing, reading, and counting. Curious little angels leaving La Milagrosa school, surrounded by nuns with such enormous headpieces they looked like flying novices ready to lift off.

Arecibo, a town of streets and smiles, alleys and slopes where public cars went up and down. A house that might not have been yours, but where they always offered you a glass of cold water so you would not reach the top "with your tongue hanging out."

For peaceful people, this city fit like a ring on a finger. Its men cut sugarcane or worked at **Cambalache** or at the Ron Rico distillery, which perfumed the air whenever you passed by. Its women worked hard at home or in textile factories. It was a town of workers and dreamers, capable of sharing a few coins with a beggar and a sincere greeting with the whole world. And although it was not proclaimed out loud, the Carnival was our patriotic pride. Once a year the city dressed itself in tradition and celebration, just in case Saint Philip the Apostle felt like escaping with the joy.

The Cathedral rose like an eternal giant, soaked by the rains of time, battered by hurricanes, shaken by earthquakes, and stubborn in remaining standing for every generation. That was not just a temple; it was a vault of memories. Witness to carnivals, to romances in the plaza, to stolen kisses, because in those days' kisses were not supposed to walk freely down the street. Around it everything changed, and there she stood, unmoving, with crossed hands and her gaze fixed on the sky. From her skirt came tentacles that turned into alleys, avenues, and neighborhoods, branches of the same heart.

In La Muy Leal Villa you found everything, streets that climbed toward **La Gloria**, others that dipped down to **El Cielo** or even to New York, and if you were not careful, there were paths that could lead you straight to hell. There were hard neighborhoods where everything was cracked or faded, places where people warned you that you might walk in alive and leave in whatever shape fate decided. They said it was dangerous, forgetting that it was also rich in culture and solidarity, a place where people fought poverty with their bare hands. Because, as someone once said, "Without housing projects and the barrios, where would the poor live?"

Arecibo, Diamond of the North, home of the lions in El Fuerte roaring through history, a miniature Statue of Liberty, Queen Elizabeth II on the Monserrate hill, avenues where you could find everything "**bonito y barato.**"

Colorful sweets like rainbows, dusted in powder from La Estrella Bakery. The smell of **empanadillas** and **bacalaítos** in the Plaza del Mercado. The old women selling food. The old men selling vegetables. From the countryside came acerolas and ripe mango, from the sea, fresh fish and salt.

Unforgettable were the slightly out of tune violins and trombones of the **Escuela Libre de Música**, and the sweet commotion of young voices from the Jefferson and the Muñoz Rivera schools, the antechamber to adult life. There was the High Vieja, the High Nueva and the Vocational School, our doors to the future. But in truth, life was learned in the hallways and during recess, which was not for playing, but for falling in love. If notebooks could speak, they would tell of verses hidden among exercises and equations, secrets kept in adolescent ink.

Within those four walls we learned that life does not come with long summer vacations. That there are things that can be taught but never truly learned. That exams measure very little. That failure is a teacher, not a sentence. That official history hides the real one. We also learned that fame is fleeting and that you can feel alone even while surrounded by a million people. Three years of adventures, anger, and joy. And the fear was never of the first day of school, but of the last. Because saying goodbye to your best friends means admitting that you may never see them again. And still, that affection stays with you forever. You may leave Dr. María Cadilla High School behind, but somehow you always find your way back... even if only in memory.

Arecibo is living history, humble Captain Correa stopping English invaders, Víctor Rojas throwing himself into the sea to save lives, and a coastline carpeted with golden sand giving birth to **La Poza del Obispo**. The Most Loyal of all towns, where the first dreams are planted, where one runs, grows, and even hopes to die old. A box of surprises, women like mermaids and others round like Mirta Silva, romantic trios singing from balconies, the salsa of Luisito Carrión and Michael Stuart, the howl of El Lobo, the Capitanes breaking the league, and the cetí, transparent and slippery, reminding us that the river also guards its miracles.

CHAPTER 5
CETI – "SEA GOLD"

E arly at dawn, Don Lino would walk down to the Río Grande de Arecibo with his net over his shoulder. The air smelled of salt and freshly brewed coffee; the tired moon hid behind the mountains. He could not delay, because he knew that was the hour when the **cetí** swam upriver. A tiny, transparent swarm moving against the current in search of life. For Don Lino every school was a miracle, an army of flickers, an aquatic procession that filled the dark water with light. He cast the net with patience, like someone extending a secret. The mesh closed, and when he pulled it back in, hundreds of little fish danced trapped inside, blinking like stars torn from the sky.

As he filled his bucket, he remembered his grandfather and his father, who had also come down to these waters on the same dawns, with the same calloused hands. Fishing for cetí was not just work; it was inheritance, ritual, a way of speaking with the dead through the river.

When he returned to the neighborhood, Doña Julia, his wife, waited for him with the pan hot and ready. The neighbors arrived with plates and laughter, and the cetí became a shared breakfast. Don Lino saved some to sell to Guayabo so he could make the best empanadas in town.

And right there, in front of the river, where the fishermen parked their little boats, stood a small wooden house painted sky blue. At its open window, with the smoke from the stove dancing with the salty breeze, Doña Tomasa spent her afternoons frying **cetí empanadas** and alcapurrias for El Guayabo, the fritura stand. The smell of fried dough mixed with the cry of seagulls, and you could smell it all the way from the Vigía bridge.

The bright, tiny cetí arrived fresh in tin buckets, brought by Don Lino and other fishermen who cast their nets just as the sun began to rise. Doña Tomasa greeted them with her usual smile and a pitcher of cold water. While she peeled green plantains and grated

yautía, she would say, "the secret is in the hand, not the recipe." And everyone in the neighborhood knew it; no alcapurria tasted like hers.

The oil hissed and bubbled as if applauding the ritual. Children and old folks rushed to grab the hottest ones, while tourists asked what kind of fish smelled like the sea and the river at the same time. "That is cetí," someone would answer, "a fish born in the sea, but that comes to live in the river."

Between empanada and empanada, Doña Tomasa told stories, about the river's floods, about nights of parranda, and about the fisherman who once promised her eternal love with a flamboyán flower. And as she spoke, she turned the empanadas with a long-handled spoon, frying them until they crackled like an applause for the past.

When the sun began to hide and the sky turned orange, Doña Tomasa turned off the stove, gathered the trays, and looked toward the river. "Tomorrow there will be more cetí and hotter alcapurrias."

The cetí is a poem, a love story in which a tiny fish lives enchanted by the glow of the moon and ends up a victim of her charms. The moon, loyal only to the fisherman, betrays him when she announces its arrival during the waning quarter so the fishermen can wait for it at the river mouth and catch it with their nets and drop it into a bucket. The fever for the "gold of the sea" keeps the fisherman awake so he can live a nighttime adventure with the sea gods and witness the beautiful sunrise of beloved Borinquen.

CHAPTER 6

THE TOWNS OF MY HOMELAND

The towns of Puerto Rico all share a family resemblance, yet each keeps a charm entirely its own. You walk into a town and already know what awaits you, the great plaza at the center with its iron benches and low flying pigeons, the church with its bell tower measuring the hours, and around it, the little shops, the pharmacy, the bakery where the scent of warm bread still drifts out the door. That heartbeat at the center is the same here, there, and everywhere across the island.

...And though they may look alike, every town carries its own soul. In Arecibo, the sea roars so close you can feel the plaza breathe salt. In Utuado, the air tastes of coffee and mountain mist. In Ponce, even the cobblestones wear their pride, and the Parque de

Bombas, dressed in its red and black stripes, guards the town like a lion. And in every plaza, when the patron saint festivities begin, no matter where you stand, you feel as if you are back in your own neighborhood. In Mayagüez the breeze smells of peanut ice cream. In Caguas the air fills with roast pork. In Bayamón the scent of chicharrón wanders through the streets.

Our towns are like first cousins, similar in shape, yet each offering a different embrace. And wherever you go, there is always a bench waiting for conversation, a lady selling **piraguas** (Puerto Rican Shaved Ice), and a tiny piece of Puerto Rico ready to greet you. That is our wealth, the comfort of what repeats itself, and the small details that make each town unmistakably its own.

Just as cousins share a grandfather's traits, the shape of the eyes, a contagious laugh, a certain stubborn streak, the towns of Puerto Rico share the same ancestral soul while keeping their own rhythm. Some are festive, others quiet, some born beside the sea with the scent of salt and coconut, others nestled in mountains waking to the perfume of freshly brewed coffee. Each one guards its own character, its own cadence, its own way of speaking, yet all of them share an invisible root, a common blood that makes us kin. Walk through them and you feel it, that familiar warmth, like arriving at a family gathering and recognizing in every face a piece of your own story. Every town carries that island heart, that mix of joy and melancholy that calls us back the way one returns to an embrace that has never stopped waiting.

To wander the streets of our towns is to flip through a weathered photo album, every corner holding a story, every balcony a watchful gaze, every corner store a small pause where time sits down to rest. The colorful facades, peeling under sun and rain, stand with the dignity of elders who have witnessed too many farewells.

Sometimes you think you have arrived in a brand-new place, but the very first greeting gives it away, the familiar accent, the simple kindness offered without asking where you come from. Deep down, Puerto Rico is a single beloved town, a song that shifts its tone but keeps the same melody. Perhaps that is why, when a traveler leaves, he carries with him a sweet nostalgia, a longing that feels like family love. Because among so many towns so alike, one never feels as if leaving a place behind, but many cousins smiling from afar, waiting for your return with a hot cup of coffee and a fresh story to share.

CHAPTER 7
THE SASSY SERVANT

A year after their first breakfast together, their love kept growing, rising at the same steady pace as his wife's little belly.

"My love, I am with child."

What a dramatic way to announce a pregnancy.

The news, as beautiful and exciting as it was, hit him like a bucket of cold water. He had no idea how to react. It felt as if she had reached into his chest and squeezed his heart like a lemon. He was about as prepared for that announcement as an atheist is for the Rapture. His stomach twisted, nausea washing over him. All he managed to do was hug her and whisper, "I hope she's a girl as beautiful as you."

With the joy of her news, he forgot to share his own: he had just lost his job. Not wanting to ruin the moment, he decided to wait until the next day to deliver the bad news.

A year and a half later, with a baby girl in his arms and still no job, another announcement arrived.

"My love, I am with child."

"Is there no other way for you to break the news?"

"Woman, people are going to think we are Guiney pigs."

"And since when do you care what people say?"

Touché. Those who fear the "what will people say" lose half their lives trapped in that thought. From across the room, he looked at the woman of his dreams, and if he had listened to "what other people say", they never would have ended up together.

Our ancestors raised us on gossip like it was a national sport. From Madame Chencha (Myrta Silva), to El Show de las 12 with Ruth Fernández, Chanita (Ángela Meyer), to La Comay, every barrio on the island of Agüeybaná had its official gossip queen. But in their neighborhood, the true capital of gossip was the church, that holy runway where the young ladies walked in all dolled up and walked out looking like they had survived a spiritual hurricane.

...And that was where the couple met the one and only SAAVY SANDUNGUERA.

The holy sandunguera always arrived right on time,

long skirt swaying, bun tight enough to survive a category five hurricane, voice ready to break into the opening chorus. But the moment the music picked up a little extra tumbao, her foot started tapping, her claps found a deeper rhythm, and suddenly the Holy Spirit seemed confused with reggaetón. The congregation watched her from the corner of their eyes, some disapproving, others wishing they had the courage to join her. She smiled because she knew her truth, servant of God, yes, but also a sandunguera at heart.

One Sunday, in the middle of service, the worship band slipped in a rhythm too delicious to ignore. The sandunguera did not even try to resist. First came the claps, then the shoulders, and before anyone could say Hallelujah, she was marking a full holy sandungueo between the pews. That was when the sandunguera, also known as the pastor's wife, caught in a trance of sacred chaos, with the bass thumping and the drums shaking the floorboards, prophesied that the young couple's marriage would not last six months.

...And the people of God said Amen. Amen, while the poor couple tried to disappear from pure embarrassment.

Amen, because in that church whatever the sandunguera said became law, no matter how ridiculous. She preached about everything that "mattered," the hair, the makeup, the jewelry, and making sure that skirt did not rise even a millimeter above the knees The altar turned into her stage, where holiness mixed with gossip and doctrine tangled itself with nonsense.

Those "services," advertised as "the glory of God," always had a start time, but never an end time. Nothing got paused, and no one dared measure anything. The show ended only when the chorus hit "hi," and the repeater kicked in with a sandungueo that made everyone shake their bones and speak in tongues that sounded freshly invented.

It was an "anointing service," the kind where women fell to the floor and trembled to the same repeating verse, reminded again and again that holiness meant long hair, long skirts, and zero makeup. Sandungueo in church was like a spark inside an incense cloud, a collision of worlds, a faith brave enough to swing its hips.

The saddest sight was the husbands watching their young wives transform overnight, "after coming to Christ," into someone who suddenly looked thirty years older. And then the congregation acted shocked when rumors of infidelity ran through the church like wildfire. But the real tragedy was not the gossip or the adultery, it was the systematic humiliation of those women. They were taught to dim their beauty, their joy, their identity. They learned to shrink because the pulpit insisted that shrinking was holy.

The result was obedience so extreme it was praised as virtue, a forced sacrifice that robbed them of intellectual, professional, and personal growth. Entire generations grew up under the rule obey first, think later, or never. That is violence too, a sophisticated violence, moralized, dressed up as holiness. Abuse wrapped in scripture, twisted interpretations, and carefully planted fear.

How is it possible that no one speaks up? Why does spiritual abuse walk around with so much impunity? Because yes, it is abuse, abuse that kills confidence, identity, and sometimes life itself.

And yet, the couple married anyway, happily, stubbornly, and full of love. The prophecy once shouted with such fervor turned out to be as false as the doctrine that tried to hold it up. The only thing that was real was the damage it caused.

CHAPTER 8

NO HARDSHIP IS ETERNAL

No hardship is eternal, and nobody is built to bear it endlessly. He reminded himself of that the year he turned twenty-three, when he finally decided to take off and move *pa' allá afuera.* He was tired, more like desperate. His wife had just given birth, with a baby girl crying for milk day and night, and another little one always clinging to her side. Love was abundant, but so was the weight of responsibility. And he knew that no hardship is eternal, although some seasons stretch themselves thin.

He never feared work, and he was no slacker. There simply was not enough to keep him busy and paid. Everything he had saved with such effort was gone, and his so-called castle, once imagined with bright hope, had shrunk into a tiny room in his in-laws' house. He felt like a stray dog seeking shelter, living in a place where even his time did not belong to him. But again, he repeated the old truth, nobody is built to bear it endlessly, and certainly not with two babies crying on opposite hips.

Living with the in-laws had its own seasoning. Sometimes it was a blessing, sometimes a torment, and always a lesson. At first the house smelled of freshly brewed coffee and *pan sobao*, the air warm with companionship and security and embrace. But soon came the long stares, the advice disguised as commandments, and that eternal question, "¿Van a llegar tarde otra vez?". It felt like living in a reality show without cameras, full of interruptions, unsolicited guidance, and comedy at every corner. And each time the house tightened around him, he reminded himself that no hardship is eternal, even when the walls feel too close.

Trouble found them quickly. Romantic nights were not so romantic. One night the bed broke, and immediately the father-in-law's voice came booming through the thin wall, "¡Turn the volume down, I work tomorrow!". They looked at each other, first frustrated, then laughing until their stomachs hurt. They learned to steal kisses in the kitchen, leave little notes under plates, and exchange secret looks while the in-laws delivered their never-ending homilies. Love, unlike hardship, does endure.

One afternoon, walking through the barrio with their fingers intertwined, he squeezed her hand and said, "¿Sabes qué, Marusha?, maybe we do not have our own house yet, but we have something better, a love that survives even with the in-laws included." Marusha smiled and kissed him right there, unafraid of witnesses or whispers. They both understood that no hardship is eternal, and no crowded house could shrink the love they were building.

At night he would sit in the rocking chair, rocking their one-year-old to sleep. He thought about his life and what it had become, and deep inside he recognized that the people who drove him crazy were also a blessing. His daughter slept, lulled by the cool mountain breeze, while he silently mourned the carefree days of childhood, when life was nothing but running across hills and kicking cans down rocky roads. "Qué tristeza la mía," he whispered, "ni siquiera vivo en mi propio barrio." But the proverb returned, no hardship is eternal, not even this chapter.

He did not sleep in his own bed, or eat at his own table, or swing in his own hammock. He was not from the mountain. He did not know how to plant **guineos, yuca**, or **batata**. He did not know the seasons of avocados or pomarrosas, or the rhythms of the harvest. His father-in-law would say, "El **puertorro** será puertorro en la costa o en el campo." And he knew the old man spoke truth. Home is not a geography, home is a feeling, and hardship is never forever.

Still, he missed the roar of the waves, the soft touch of warm foam, and the sand massaging between his toes. Maybe the man of the mountains could not understand how the sea spoke through a seashell, carrying music only the soul could hear. The ocean was a giant witness to the divine, a horizon with no beginning and no end, a keeper of stories, lovers, conquerors, freedom, shipwrecks, fishermen, sirens. Hardship comes and goes, but the sea remains faithful.

He looked around at the endless green. The wind was soft and melodic, playing with the flowers. A tired breeze drifted down the mountain. Birds sang in the sky, waterfalls answered inside the forest. In the mountain it rained and rained and rained, and with the rain came the perfume of wet blossoms. Rivers formed from water rolling down steep peaks, slipping into hidden creeks and natural pools. Nature reminded him, in its quiet way, that hardship is never eternal, even when the rain feels endless.

In the countryside the nightingale was king, the **pitirre** ruled the skies, and spring reigned all year.

Paths bloomed with butterflies. Trees seemed to wear new leaves every week. The air smelled of coffee and guava. Bamboo forests swayed like orchestras of bolero. From the mouths of caves came mysterious sounds, but no one followed them, not with bats and snakes and spiders lurking in the dark.

At dusk people tended their gardens, their rose-bushes, their climbing vines. And at night the **coquí** sang to the moon without rest. In the morning the fog wrapped everything in silver, making him feel as if he lived inside a cloud. On the coast the moon appeared rounder, but in the countryside, she glowed more silver. In both places he sensed the same unchanging truth, hardship may fall like rain, but it never falls forever.

Late one night, when everyone had gone to bed, he overheard his father-in-law talking through the thin wooden walls, walls that had ears and revealed every secret.

"Woman, I don't know what that stubborn boy has, but I like him."

"Maybe you just like someone who talks back to you."

"That boy is sharp. He's not a fool like my other sons-in-laws.

"So, tell me, why does he have to go so far away?"

"Things of life, woman. It's just that in this country the pineapple is sour.

And hearing that, he realized that the pineapples had always been sour for Puerto Ricans. He would not be the first nor the last to leave in search of a better life. Puerto Ricans had been leaving since Puerto Ricans were Puerto Ricans.

After the 1898 invasion many abandoned their lands and headed to Cuba and the Dominican Republic. After hurricane San Ciriaco in 1899 hunger drove thousands to Hawaii to cut cane under near-slavery conditions. The diaspora was older than him, older than his father, older than his father's father. It was a cycle of hardship, but he knew the truth well by now. No hardship is eternal. Not for him, and not for his people.

And somewhere between the song of the *coquí* and the tired sigh of the mountain wind, he understood. He would survive this chapter too. Because no hardship is eternal, and nobody is built to bear it endlessly.

CHAPTER 9
VOICES FROM THE COUNTRYSIDE

One morning, while walking through the countryside, he was interrupted by the sound of galloping. It was Margaro coming up the slope, riding his horse Fuego. What a character old Margaro was. There are not many like him left. He was the last harvest of the Puerto Rican jíbaro, the soul of our island, a mix of nobility, hard work, simple wisdom, love for the land, and a good sense of humor.

Margaro wore a straw hat and a white shirt tied at the neck with a red bandana. He paired it with loose khaki pants tucked into large black boots. He carried a machete in his hand that glimmered every time the sun touched it. He was built like a bull, and his voice was loud and proud. His hair was white, his eyes green, and he had horse-like teeth that had never felt the touch of a toothbrush.

Margaro was not educated and he was illiterate, yet he was full of natural wisdom. He could read the sky, he knew the song of the coquí as if it were his clock, and he recognized the shift in the wind just by watching the leaves of the plantain tree. He was content with the little he had. He woke up before sunrise, whistling softly while the rooster announced the day. When he spoke, he did so in proverbs. He often said he was poor, stubborn, and proud, lacking resources, but rich in dignity and virtue. His hands were rough, yet soft when he planted, and his face showed the marks of hard work, but he always carried a smile ready to give. He lived in a small wooden house with tiny rooms, and he claimed to be happy because he lacked nothing. He spoke about working the soil, milking a cow, and homemade remedies to cure the flu. He said that a true jíbaro does not complain, he prays, he gets up, and he keeps going. He knew how to roast a pig on the spit. He was not afraid of work, he would sell you a bunch of plantains, clear out a backyard, or cut cane. No one was more skilled on horseback. He greeted everyone with his tobacco clicking between his teeth, "God bless you, my saint", and continued on his way singing...

♪ ...La Loma del Tamarindo...♪

Farther along, a bright-eyed old woman shouted to get his attention. She looked about seventy, gray-haired and thin, with the sturdy posture of someone who had battled the land her whole life and won. She lived in a tiny wooden house, barely one room, and her voice rang out from the small steps in front. It was Doña Luz, waving him over like she had been expecting him.

He had to climb a small slope and, hesitantly, he approached the little house, surrounded by a fence made of red and yellow hibiscus bushes. The elderly woman had something in her hand that she was offering with great enthusiasm.

She was a tiny woman. She wore an old floral dress that fell below her knees. From a distance she looked much frailer than when standing close to her. Her hair, like a net of silver thread, covered her head and shone under the sun. Her face was wrinkled, but the lines made her look sweet. Something about her made him feel at home. The way she stood, her slightly bent back, and her eyes full of tenderness reminded him of his own grandmother.

In her gentle hand she held a little paper cone filled with small pieces of white ice.

"Come here muchacho, try my coconut **limbers**."

"Oh señora, but I did not bring any money."

"Who said anything about money, it is a little gift, take it."

Doña Luz would not accept a "no" for an answer, and he had no choice but to extend his hands and receive her gift.

"Go on young man, taste it before it melts."

He leaned against the wooden house to hide from the sun, under the shade of a breadfruit tree, and tasted the sweet treat she had given him. As he enjoyed the refreshing limber, he could not help glancing inside the little house. It was dark, but rays of sunlight came through the small wooden windows and the gaps in the walls. It seemed that all of Doña Luz's possessions were in a tiny corner of the house beside a bed. There were pots and pans on a small sink in front of the window. On a small table there were several cans of food. The old woman's face lit up with the warmest and brightest smile as he ate the limber.

"What do you think, young man?"

"It is delicious."

"Thank you, tomorrow come by to try the passion fruit and pineapple ones."

He was astonished. He thought she was extraordinary. Here was a woman who had barely enough to eat and little else. Yet she was offering a perfect stranger the best of what she had, a gift without conditions and full of kindness, expecting nothing in return.

How can someone who lives in complete poverty, with so few possessions, still be so happy, so trusting, so full of joy, so generous, and so willing to share? Perhaps life was teaching him that there are wealthy people with almost nothing, and poor people who have everything.

From childhood we are taught to share because generosity is something we learn. But sharing is an art, and like all good art, it must be developed. From the moment we cling to our mother's chest, we come out screaming that everything is "mine". Yet in the barrio when we give something, we give all of it, because it is more blessed to give than to receive.

He said goodbye to Doña Luz with thanks and a huge smile. He knew this was the beginning of a beautiful friendship.

Down the road lived Margarita, if you can call that living. She grew up too soon. As the oldest, childhood skipped over her and she was forced to work tirelessly every day, caring for her younger siblings while her parents worked and became slaves to poverty. As a child she carried a heavy burden on her shoulders. Her work never stopped, not even at sunset. In her teenage years she already felt like an old woman, thin and with tired little eyes. She had no time to go to school. She would not leave her home. She would not have friends. She would not marry. She would never escape her life. A bad hand was dealt to her because she was the first-born, and she was not enslaved by a person, but by a life from which it was impossible to break free. All that work earned her stares, mockery, and judgment, along with the nickname "**la jamona**" of the barrio, which later became the label of the old-maid aunt.

We do not always know what to call that kind of life. Maybe it is a kind of child abuse. The fact that people often did not understand it does not make it right. The scars remain the same. Maybe that is why she loved flowers so much. Every time she saw a cut flower, she knew exactly how it felt. It had no roots, nothing anchoring it to the world, yet it was still expected to give its best, its beauty, its warmth, and to brighten the hearts of others. She was a Puerto Rican Cinderella who could only dream.

Many times, she wanted to scream that she was not the mother, that she was not responsible, but she never found the courage to do it, and the years passed.

Now her parents and siblings are gone. She lives alone in the blue house, where the air always smells of fresh coffee and jasmine at the window. The house she inherited from her parents now feels spacious to her.

People say the ship of love sailed right past her because of her temperament, but she does not care what they say. She has the smile of someone who has seen everything and needs no one's approval. She lives an ordinary life, but she finds flavor in it. She keeps her hair pulled back and a sparkle in her eyes that time does not dare to dim. Her clothing is simple, usually a white blouse and skirts in gray or black. Children look for her because she tells stories, although some say she is a witch. Cats follow her because she understands them, and the neighbors envy her because she does whatever she wants without asking anyone's permission.

The house is surrounded by beautiful shrubs and trees. She cares for her flowers with the same tenderness she once had for her little siblings. The yard is her sanctuary and her place of peace. She never said why she did not marry, except in the form of a joke, "I did not have time". She is not alone, she simply chose peace, memories, and a good book as her companions. She could probably have married if she wanted to, but we will never know for sure because she is not interested in answering those questions. She has better things to do with her time, like tending her flowers and baking delicious cookies.

CHAPTER 10
MISFIT ANGELS

He walks down the slope, looks to both sides of the neighborhood, and chooses to walk uphill toward the center of the community. He snaps off a little stick from a rosewood tree in case he needs to scare off a dog.

The deeper he goes into the mountain, the poorer the neighborhood looks. It is as if it offers two faces of life, one of poor people and another of people even poorer.

Every jíbaro he meets gives him a smile. "Have a good day," they say. Don Luis, the old man who sells lottery tickets, offers him a couple of numbers. He claims he has good luck, that he should buy at least one ticket, even if it is just a dollar. Don Luis walks with his bundle of tickets held together by a rubber band, wearing worn-out shoes and a shirt soaked in sweat, but in his eyes there is the certainty that he sells more than a number, he sells the possibility of a miracle.

"Man, I do not even have enough to drop dead," he replies, while thinking deep inside, "with my luck, I would not get electrocuted even if I grabbed a live wire."

The old man, disappointed that he could not make a sale, keeps walking down the slope and says goodbye with a soft smile and a shrug.

Along that path of stone streets and red mud appears Panchita, an elderly woman who always walked around with a broom, sweeping the neighborhood streets. She walked in a worn dress, covered in the dust raised by her old straw broom. When she was around the neighborhood, she did not wear shoes, only using them when she needed to take the public bus to town. Often, she carried water in a tin can balanced on her head. Old age had turned her into a keeper of trinkets.

Panchita was simply a slave of habit. Every day she repeated the same route, uphill and downhill. The stains on her cheeks and forehead framed a face that carried expressions of sadness. No one knows if she was ever beautiful, we only knew her in her present condition, the old crazy lady with the broom. She walked through life as if time owed her flowers and a pair of new flip-flops that clapped like war drums. He was afraid to greet her, because she was pure fire hidden in wrinkles. Panchita did not talk to anyone; her greeting was simply an angelic smile.

He could not help wondering why people look down on "crazy old ladies." They are the ones who care for stray dogs, for the cats in the alley, or like Panchita, who sweep simply because they want everything clean. They forget names, but never emotions. They talk to themselves, to the plants or the cats, but in truth they are talking to time, to old friends who are gone, and to the little girl they still carry inside.

A few meters ahead, in front of the parish, he runs into Tinito. He probably was not as old as his worn appearance suggested. His nickname described him perfectly. He was small, slightly hunched, and looked unkempt. He carried a sack everywhere, where he kept bottles, cans, and anything he could sell for a few cents. Better to sell cans than to sell your soul. With dirty clothes, a long beard, and his bags of a wanderer, he walked bent over, with no clear destination, always looking at the ground. At best he was invisible to the rest of the neighborhood, and at worst, the indifference he received pushed him deeper into his ruined madness. Maybe the short-brimmed hat he always wore, full of holes, was part of a disguise that helped him feel invisible.

People who saw him on the street looked and kept walking as if he did not exist. He watched them from afar and hurried his step. It was better to keep distance, just in case it was one of those days he woke up crazier than ever and confused you with one of the "hoodlums" of the barrio and hit you with a blow. Even so, the kids could not resist the temptation to tease him. The mothers used his appearance to turn him into the "boogeyman" when children refused to eat or misbehaved.

"If you do not eat, Tinito will come and carry you away in his sack."

Why are there so many "crazy" people? Maybe the Divine loves them because they are not afraid to be happy, because in their so-called madness lives purity, laughter, hope, and a small piece of heaven. Maybe the Divine understands them because they have been as misunderstood as the things we cannot see.

He felt a soft déjà vu, as if, for a moment, he were walking through his own barrio again. The faces were different, yes, but the free spirits were the same. Back home the man who walked with a box balanced on his head was Belto. And Belto, by the way, was not crazy at all. He had made it his mission to prove he could carry anything on his head, anything: boxes, cans, bottles, buckets of water, a gallon of milk, a dozen eggs, sacks of rice, even sacks of cement, whatever you dared to hand him.

What made Belto unforgettable was that he moved through the streets "faster than nature," which made him the perfect candidate for every errand in the barrio. He talked just as fast as he walked, with an attention span that flickered like a match in the wind. But with his humility, his eagerness to help, and that smile capable of breaking the grumpiest face wide open, he earned the affection of everyone who knew him.

If a free-spirited soul is someone who brings joy wherever they go, then **Tita the Fierce** was eccentric in the most glorious way. Without a doubt she was the most beloved character in the barrio. For her there were no strangers. She knew everyone by name and greeted each person with a shout loud enough to echo from one end of the neighborhood to the other. What a set of lungs she had, giving you plenty of time to either welcome her in or hurry to close the door. When Tita arrived at any house, the entire barrio knew it.

Tita carried joy like a lantern. People used her quirks to live out, through her, the things they themselves lacked the courage to do. She sang, she danced, she celebrated life with no brakes and no shame. If you wanted a dose of happiness, you only had to look at her. The happiest people in the barrio were always the so-called "crazy ones." They spoke of flying, even though we all knew humans cannot fly.

They were artists, making masterpieces out of brooms and aluminum cans rescued from the trash. They were fashion designers, dressing themselves in elegance with every mismatched piece of clothing the neighbors donated. They were poets, sitting in silence to listen to melodies no composer had ever written and to words no poet had ever dared to speak. People called them crazy only because they dared to be different. They were not crazy because they lost their minds, but because someone had stolen them long ago. Maybe that is why they always seemed to be searching for something.

Some lived trapped inside their own heads, yet somehow, they were freer than all of us. For them every day was a celebration, every day a Social Friday, a Dancing Saturday, or a Recovery Sunday. They were **gritty angels**, messy and miraculous, making our lives brighter with every one of their beautiful, bewildering antics.

The "free spirited" do not sleep under roofs like ours. Their ceiling is the open sky, sometimes filled with stars, sometimes covered by clouds, sometimes replaced by a cardboard box beneath a bridge. And somehow, they handle the world better than we do, facing the scorching midday sun or the cold rain of winter while we rest warm under walls that never test us.

They prefer animals and the animals prefer them. Perhaps because cats and dogs do not get scared when they receive tenderness. They think we are the crazy ones. The sane do not understand them because they play with dolls while we play with people's feelings. We get upset that they do not know how to lie and instead rub salt in our wounds with the truth. Some of them speak slower than us, others speak as fast as a speeding bullet. They see what we cannot see. To the sensible, the crazy ones drive cars without wheels, sail ships that do not float, and fly planes that never leave the ground. Maybe that is why they never get bored.

Some are crazy from sadness and pain. Others had their hearts broken. Life has dealt them too many blows. They try to disconnect to forget reality. Some shout merely to keep people away, they only want their space respected. They prefer to live alone in their fantastic world. We know very little about them, and the truth is that we are not really interested in knowing more. They are like skunks, and they use their smell as a defense mechanism.

We should not forget that these joyful souls have the same right as anyone to live in the neighborhood, walk its streets, and enter the store.

The truth is that every family has something dysfunctional. There is an old saying that goes, "Of poets, fools, and crazy people, we all have a little."

A FEATHERED CLOCK

In the countryside the rooster woke you before dawn. He could never understand how Florindo, a rooster with bright multicolored feathers, was born with such perfect timing. Florindo was energetic and defiant. Every single day at daybreak that feathered alarm clock marched out to sound his call. "Compay, yoke the ox, the day is about to break." That rooster seemed like a soldier with a bugle. He crowed loudly, with a sharp and endless cry that traveled across the hills.

He was not used to waking up to a rooster, but for the campesino the crowing of that bird was more beautiful than church bells. The handsome creature stretched its neck to welcome the morning, believing that if it did not sing the sun would refuse to rise. Its call carried the smell of freshly brewed coffee and the aroma of vegetables that would soon become the campesino's lunch.

What bothered him most about the rooster was not only that it chased sleep away, but that it dragged him from the warm little body of his wife, from that soft patch of skin that sheltered his soul every night. On the coldest mountain mornings Marusha was a living stove, a fire that never failed him. When she sweated, her back carried the scent of tropical flowers, warm and intoxicating. Her firm, rounded hips were a perfect refuge, a place where a man in love could cling like a limpet and forget the world.

But that meddling rooster existed only to throw him out of his nest of love. It annoyed him so deeply that chasing it away became a nightly ritual. Every evening before bed he lined up a handful of stones on top of the wardrobe, ready to launch the moment the rooster opened its beak. "Damn rooster, go bother the hens and let me sleep in peace," he would grumble into the cold dawn.

Once the battle with the rooster began there was no returning to sleep. All his senses were wide awake. For the campesino the rooster's crow signaled the start of another good day. For him it was the start of another heavy one. Now the world poured in: children crying somewhere down the valley, the squeaks of nestlings waking in the brush, the neighbors' pigs grunting, and the thunderous engine of Juan López's public bus grinding up the mountain. And worse than all the noise were his own thoughts, restless and burdened. That rooster did not just wake the countryside, it reminded him cruelly that another day had begun, and another day had arrived without work.

On the coast you did not wake up to a rooster, but to WKAQ, because not all of us have the neighbor we wish we had.

You had barely opened your eyes, minding your own sleepy thoughts, when suddenly the whole house trembled and the voice of Fernando Pérez González burst through the window like an uninvited relative.

"♪ La gran noticia de la hora ♪"

The floor vibrated under the weight of pure inconsideration, yet the voices of those men and women born to speak through radio waves echoed throughout the entire neighborhood. Whether you liked it or not, WKAQ delivered the news straight into your bones.

Radio was how people talked to the world. It was not only the cheapest form of entertainment, for many it was the only one. The radio was always there, steady as a lighthouse, offering precise reports, politics, gossip, and sports. It was the grandmother listening to Mass, the neighbor glued to a baseball game, the teenager waiting to hear the latest hit. If your house did not have a television, the radio was your living room.

We learned to love baseball with Paracorto Andújar and Ernesto Díaz González, and basketball with the eternal Captain, Eddie Jové. Those of us who cherished music laughed and swayed with Rafita González. The radio made us cry with soap operas filled with impossible romances, illegitimate children, vengeance, hatred, and betrayal. Alfred D. Herger kept us entertained, but the real laughter belonged to Tres Patines. And when the moment felt right, you found yourself singing along, loud and proud.

The radio brought hope. It brought songs, new and old, that tasted like childhood. The radio was like changing a baby's diaper, it did not solve your problems forever, but for a moment it made life gentler. And unlike the rooster, you could not throw rocks at it.

CHAPTER 12

OLD FRIENDS FROM THE NEIGHBORHOOD

He liked climbing to the top of the mountain. Sitting under an avocado tree he could see the valley, the whole town, and if there was no fog he could even catch a glimpse of the beach. Solitude and distance had become his companions. He was an observant man, and he often spent hours watching people walk past the house. He entertained himself following the flight of a guaraguao that, like a black cross, circled between the clouds. He watched it until it disappeared, diving into the forest to trap some helpless prey in its claws.

When he looked down he saw the flatlands cut in two by the river. In the distance the cows continued chewing their eternity, and over their backs, white and curious specks, the egrets searched for ticks as if nothing could disturb the calm of the countryside.

When he extended his gaze toward the horizon he could see the entire coast. He closed one eye to aim at the distance and, as if looking through a telescope, bring closer the place where his barrio sat. From the lighthouse to the left was the town, and from the lighthouse to the right was the place where he was raised.

The barrio where he was born lay in front of the sea, a fishermen's neighborhood surrounded by palm trees, icacos, and sea grape bushes. During the day it was covered by a blue sky with cotton-like clouds, adorned by flamboyanes and blooming almond trees. The sun punished it with a suffocating fury. In the afternoon it was caressed by the sea breeze and fanned by the palms that swayed sensually like women with their hair down, dancing to a melody whispered by seashells. At night it dressed in elegance, wrapped in stars, and the moon looked so close you wanted to reach out and touch it. When it rained the water ran down the stone streets toward the lower areas, forming muddy puddles that looked like lakes of chocolate.

He loved the feeling of being a giant, watching the world spread beneath him, holding up his fingers to measure the shape of things as if he could pinch mountains or balance the whole valley on his thumb. And for a moment he imagined God above, looking down at him with the same quiet curiosity.

Out there, wrapped in the hush of nature, he understood that the divine is not somewhere else, it is life itself. And he wondered, who is our neighbor? Only the ones who walk on two legs? Or also the soil beneath our feet, the trees that breathe for us, the plants that feed us, the animals that keep us company, the birds and the fish, the rivers and the seas, the air we borrow and the wind that returns it to us?

He leaned against the tree, pulled his knees to his chest, and in the distance the memories of his childhood rose before his eyes like a small film.

We have all been children. That is true, and no one escapes that.

All those hours playing with friends, riding bicycles, exploring the hills, sneaking off to the beach, or begging permission to go to the plaza, it seemed like our only task was to be happy.

Growing up in the barrio meant playing marbles or bottle caps in the middle of the street or throwing yourself down the Vigía hill in a homemade bolines cart. We were poor, so we made the carts ourselves. One plank, two axles, four ball-bearing wheels, and a piece of rope to steer. No engine needed, because the magic was in the hill. And off you went down that mountain of asphalt, no helmet, no kneepads. You had no brakes, so you stopped with your feet, dragging your sneakers until they wore out, or you threw yourself onto the grass at the bottom.

But it was never the destination that mattered, it was the ride. The wind on your face and your heart beating like a drum. It was pure freedom, laughter mixed with shouts of excitement. The neighbors watched from their balconies, some worried about your safety and others smiling, remembering their own childhood. The street was an improvised racetrack, carts racing to see which rolled down the fastest, even though everyone knew the real prize was the shared experience.

In the countryside, in the barrio, or in public housing, the same story repeated itself. It was a childhood without screens, full of laughter, scraped knees, and grand adventures. That wooden cart was not a cart, it was an airplane that took us straight to adventure.

You had so much fun you forgot the time, and when night came you heard your mother's shout.

"**Fulanito**, it is time to come inside."

Time passed and you did not answer because you were too entertained.

"Fulanito, for the love of God, I told you to come inside."

Now you answered, because that was the surest way to avoid a good **cocotazo**.

Our specialty was dangerous toys. The bolines cart, the bottle-cap gun, slingshots made from tree branches, sharp-tipped spinning tops. They were dangerous, they caused bumps, scratches, and sometimes tears. Occasionally you ended up in the emergency room. But they taught us how to fall, how to get up, and how not to fear adventure.

Forget choking hazards. We are talking hot plates, toxic fumes, sharp metal objects, explosives, and the Mosquito Man. Ever run behind the fumigation truck spraying the whole neighborhood? Foolishness of the highest order.

And for breakfast we had Tang, that orange powder you mixed with water that magically became a disgustingly sweet orange juice. A chemical junk bomb where the first ingredient was sugar, followed by sugar, and more sugar. But the sweetness was not only in the sugar, but it was also in memories of a time when everything simple tasted like glory.

And as if that was not dangerous enough, we could not escape secondhand smoke. At home, in cars, on airplanes, we inhaled more secondhand smoke than the Cambalache power plant. Not to mention drinking water straight from the tap, tasting our pet's croquetas, sticking our tongue on batteries, playing with matches, sharp-tipped trompos, cap guns, bikes with no brakes, and skates without helmets or pads. We waged galactic wars on the swings. It is a miracle we survived childhood. The memories came alive in his mind like the pages of a beloved storybook.

You could travel the world, meet a million fabulous people with interesting lives and incredible achievements, and none could replace childhood friends. There was a special bond that united us, called mischief. We ran into grandma's house covered in sweat to get a glass of Tang. We hid in each other's homes when our parents chased us to give us a beating. Trees became great castles to conquer. The hills were our secret hideouts. The mangroves were enchanted lands guarded by defeated crabs. Dirt clods were our roller coasters. With the sun beating down, wind in our hair, often barefoot to avoid ruining our only pair of sneakers, and without a helmet, we threw ourselves down the hill in our homemade bolines carts. We were always busy, pumped with adrenaline, shouting, laughing, and sometimes crying with scraped knees. But every second became a memory in our story.

Old friends are not simply friends, they are part of your soul. They helped erase pain, dry your tears, make you laugh, and they were never too busy for you. If you fought with one, you fought with all. They would sneak out with you at the worst moment and were brutally honest when needed. We had a friend for every nickname: the Fat One, the Skinny One, the Tall One, the Snotty One, and unforgettable, the Fart Shooter. The one who could time a fart perfectly was considered the master of laughter. He was like a secret weapon you saved for the most necessary moments.

Thinking of childhood friends warms the soul. Not the ones who passed by occasionally, but the intimate ones from childhood, the ones you shared mischief with, your meals, even your bed. The ones who burst into uncontrollable laughter over any foolish thing. You remember special moments, their sincere eyes, their arms helping you up after a fall. You remember sitting together in silence, staring at the horizon, or drawing in the sand with a stick. All you have to do is close your eyes and see us again on our old street, in shorts, a T-shirt, and dirty sneakers, in search of the next adventure.

We were not so poor that we had no shoes, but we loved walking barefoot. We did it because we liked the tickle of grass under our feet, because it was easier than socks and laces.

Walking barefoot was one of life's pleasures, whether on stones, heat, rocks, cold, water, dirt, grass, or at the shore. Everything feels simpler barefoot, as if happiness comes directly through the soles. Grandma said we would get worms, but truth is we got sick less often. Bare feet were a symbol of innocence and strength. We walked rocky paths and kicked up clouds of dust. We endured the pain of sharp stones until our feet toughened, and the next stone did not hurt as much. Calluses were our trophies.

We mastered the art of walking barefoot. We had to do it carefully, like bomb technicians detecting small holes, imperfections, pebbles, the heat of asphalt, the bite of scorching sand. You hopped, skipped, walked on tiptoes. Your eyes scanned the ground for danger or soggy tobacco wads. Your toes were tiny sensors. Even then, walking barefoot was both amazing and intimidating, as if life challenged you from the ground up.

But the best of the best was walking barefoot on the beach. At first the sand felt like burning lava. You ran, hopped, and sank your feet until you reached the shore. The sea kissed your feet, making small bubbles and tickling you, while the breeze caressed your face. The waves rolled over your feet giving you a massage of sand and coral. The foam danced over your toes while the sun filled you with energy. Your toes moved in the water while the waves sang. You never realized you were having an almost ecstatic experience.

A downpour did not ruin the day, it opened a new channel of fun. We loved the rain. Once soaked, there was nothing left but to jump in puddles. One foot, both feet, until muddy water flew everywhere. We shouted and laughed at our brilliant idea of jumping in the mud. You needed no words for others to know you were the happiest person in the world. The joy spoke for itself. Rain fell, earth soaked, and we laughed without end. Water was magic in tiny drops.

We had no time to talk about adult things, but surely, we each kept some ambition tucked away inside. Maybe deep down we knew that pursuing our dreams came with a price that could not be measured in dollars and cents. The cost was childhood and separation, and we were not ready to talk about that. We wanted to do everything together, and for the moment that was enough. Back then we were as happy as a monkey in a banana grove.

With old friends you never remember how the friendship started. It is as if the universe united you in a moment of time and space to keep each other company. Friendship is a bond, an alliance between two people willing to walk over nails for you.

If you sit under a tree and think about your old friends, you will surely cry. Old friends remind us of what it felt like not to be who we are now.

CHAPTER 13
WHEN THE SEA BECOMES WOOD

In the barrio, long before the sun peeked over the mountain, the footsteps of the fishermen could already be heard. The first to head out was Don Pedro, better known as El Negro, a strong man with broad shoulders and skin tanned by years of sun and salt. His face, traced with deep lines, carried the wisdom of the sea and the calm of someone who had learned to read the winds. His hands, large and rough, seemed carved from wood and water at the same time. Behind him came his sons, Ito and Peyongo.

Ito was tall and slender, with a quiet gaze and a slow, steady walk. He had the bearing of someone who listened more than he spoke. Peyongo, on the other hand, wore a constant easy smile and always carried a mischievous spark in his eyes, as if life were one long, good joke. They carried the damp nets, the bait bucket, and a reverent silence broken only by the murmur of the waves.

The sea woke up calm, with that glow that makes it seem as if the world is holding its breath. The three men pushed the wooden boat, the same one El Negro had built with his own hands, and slowly slipped into the blue. Out there, surrounded by salty breeze and the golden reflections of dawn, time stood still. Negro gave instructions in a low voice, and the sons followed with the precision learned from years of watching him.

When they reached the right spot, they cast the **chinchorro**, that great net woven with patience through many winter nights. They threw it over the water the way one extends an embrace. The movement was coordinated, almost ritual. El Negro held one end, Ito adjusted the sinkers, and Peyongo kept an eye on the floats that marked the circle. With each pull of the net, the sea answered with its own rhythm, returning the fruit of their waiting.

It was a ritual repeated without fail, like a prayer of the people. And when the sun rose higher and the nets filled with sardines, snappers, groupers and **chillos,** El Negro returned to the pier with a smile only the sea could draw.

As the boat approached the shore, the people of the barrio came out to greet them. The children were always the first to arrive, splashing in the shallows, while the men hurried in to help pull the chinchorro, curious to see the silver shimmer of the catch.

Voices mixed with laughter and shouts:

"Look at that grouper!" someone would say.

"And that red snapper, what a beautiful red color!" another replied.

It became a small event, an improvised celebration gifted by the sea. In those moments, everyone shared in the abundance, the smell of salt, and the simple joy of watching their own return home with full hands.

Later, as evening fell and the barrio smelled of fresh fish and café colao, those same men transformed.

In the small workshop behind their house, El Negro, Ito, and Peyongo became artisans. With pieces of wood gathered from the mountain or the pier, they carved fish, Wise Men, and miniature boats. The same hands that hours earlier had battled the tide now moved gently over the wood, as if each shaving were a wave tamed.

Ito, with his serene expression, had the patience of a listener. He could spend hours sanding a figure until it shone like wet sand. Peyongo, with his strong arms and contagious laugh, was the creative one. He added bright colors, painted the eyes of the Wise Men, and invented stories for each figure. Negro watched them with quiet pride, remembering the days when his own father taught him that a man should know how to build both his boat and his destiny.

The neighbors often stopped by to buy a carving or simply to chat. In that small patio, among shavings, laughter, and the smell of the sea, the soul of the barrio was alive. It was not uncommon for a curious tourist to leave with one of those pieces, unaware that they were carrying a small fragment of history.

The sea gave them sustenance, but the wood gave them purpose. In both worlds, the one of waves and the one of tools, Negro and his sons had learned the same craft: creating with their hands, resisting through art.

When the sun slipped behind the cliff and the sound of the hammer blended with the song of the coquíes, Ito would often say,

"Viejo, the sea and the wood are almost the same... one gives fish, the other gives memories."

Negro would smile without looking up, while the aroma of café colao wrapped itself into the evening air.

And so, between nets, chinchorros, and wood shavings, a legacy was forged that still endures: the legacy of the men of the barrio who knew how to understand the language of the sea and the language of the wood. Men who, without knowing it, were carving the memory of a people.

CHAPTER 14
THE SOUNDS OF STEEL

I f anything defines our culture, if anything explains who we Puerto Ricans are, it is our gift for turning any street corner into a celebration, any stray sound into music, and any ordinary moment into a reason to rejoice in life. In the middle of our simplicity, rhythm gathers us, names us, and whispers where we come from.

In the barrio, music did not rise from grand stages or polished instruments. It was born in the backyard, in the workshop, in old barrels and new dreams. When the month of the fiestas patronales arrived, the steel bands claimed the streets, turning the air into a drum and the heart into rhythm.

Luis was the soul of one of those bands. He used to say that steel had memory, that every strike on the drum kept a secret of the barrio. Some claimed that Luis carried that rhythm from Loíza, learned as a boy among **bombas** and **plenas**, watching how the people there turned drumming into a kind of prayer. He brought the beat in his blood and the smile in his soul. He showed everyone that rhythm is not something you learn, it is something you inherit.

In Doña Elisa's patio, surrounded by tools, plastic chairs, and the scent of **fritura**, a small group gathered each afternoon to rehearse. They had no sheet music. They listened to each other, to the soul, to the pulse of the people.

The drums, carved from recycled oil barrels, gleamed under the sun like mirrors of another time. With hammers and fire, Luis shaped them until they could sing, each with its own voice, high or deep or raspy, yet all sharing the same fierce spirit. And when they began to play, the entire barrio awakened.

The metallic sound traveled between houses, bouncing against walls, slipping through open windows. Children ran toward the music, women swayed their shoulders from the balconies, and the men smiled with memories of their own youth. There was no stage greater than the corner and no audience more loyal than the barrio.

Luis lifted his hand and gave the signal. In an

instant, chaos softened into rhythm, and rhythm bloomed into communion. The steel bands were the steady heart of the people, the way everyone declared, "Here we are, still alive." They played at fiestas, processions, birthdays, and even funerals, because even in sorrow, life still required music.

Each drum had a name, a story. One barrel had traveled from St. Croix in a cousin's luggage, another had once held oil down at the pier. Luis knew every drum like family. And when one broke, it was never discarded. It was patched, welded, and brought back to life.

We sat on the sidewalk until the sky turned red and the air smelled of rain and **bacalaítos.** Something in that sound, that blend of metal, sweat, and joy, felt like nothing else. It was the sound of a people who refused to surrender, who turned toil and weariness into celebration.

In time, some left, and others grew old, leaving their drums resting in quiet corners. But on the happiest days, you could still hear the faint echo of that band. Somewhere in the barrio, an old drum would ring again, as if Luis himself were there, marking the beat with his smile and his hammer.

And so, with steel pulses and youthful laughter, the barrio forged another memory: the memory of those who found in music the echo of their own joy, and in steel, the indestructible strength of their spirit.

Luis always carried a seashell in his pocket, found long ago at La Poza. He kept it to remind himself that rhythm lived not only in metal, but also in water. He promised, with few words, that every Vispera de San Juan he would be on the shore with the cooler ready and the steel drums tuned to play.

The seashell in Luis's pocket grew heavy with memory. That was how the journey began, the one that became a ritual through the years. The Eve of Saint John the Baptist, when the music of the barrio found its echo in the breaking waves and the old spirit of tradition.

CHAPTER 15

THE EVE OF SAN JUAN BAUTISTA

June 23 arrived like an old promise. The cousins headed to the beach early to save a good spot for the rest of the family and to make sure the night found them all together.

The sand, at that hour, was warm and welcomed their bare feet with a joyful caress. The salt stuck to their skin as if the sea wanted to give them a welcome kiss. At the entrance stood Maggie, along with the Amigos de la Poza del Obispo, raising signs and voices against the privatization of the Poza. Between drums and firm chants, the shouts echoed:

"The Poza is not for sale! The beaches belong to the people!"

The wind, like an accomplice, carried those words

to the sea, and for a moment the waves seemed to answer with a roar of approval.

They marked their territory: the cooler between chairs, an umbrella arguing with the wind, and a music box. The Poza, with its playful waves, called to them, and they dove in, eager to squeeze every second that the day was offering them.

Later the adults arrived with food and coolers full of drinks. Bottles of Coca-Cola passed from hand to hand like fizzy little oaths, and the smell of sunscreen mixed with the tide and with the promise of not growing up too fast.

Sergio lifted his bottle in an adolescent toast:

"For the ones who came, the ones who are missing, and the ones who are always late."

The laughter that followed sealed a quick, honest truce. Migue, with hands as coordinated as two left feet, tried building a sandcastle worthy of a postcard, but it ended up looking like a sad little lump that immediately surrendered to the tide. Joshua set out to build a miniature Capitol Building and somehow produced a pyramid that clearly had delusions of grandeur. Lula, the only competent one in the group, decorated the leaning walls with seashells she found along the shore, as if good accessories could save the architecture. And when the first wave stole Migue's "castle," everyone doubled over laughing, fully aware that losing was half the fun.

Not long after, she appeared, like a foreign verse that somehow fit. Her name was Emily, an American girl wearing a university T-shirt and a huge hat to protect herself from the sun. She walked with a mix of shyness and pride, taking pictures and studying the formation of the Poza as if learning a new lesson. Next to her was Dani, her exchange partner, with an easy smile and Spanish still under construction. Dani had met Emily at school and brought her to the Poza to show her something that, according to him, "you cannot learn in class."

The boys invited them without much ceremony. Emily asked if the Poza was safe; they replied naturally that to them the beach was the best swimming pool in the world. Emily blended in quickly: she tried frituras, learned clumsy salsa steps, and laughed at the jokes Joshua made in his sandal-flavored English. Dani, proud of his role as host, tried to translate jokes and correct his own English with tenderness.

The day brought its share of charming disasters. Migue, trying to impress, ran and jumped into the water with the intention of a heroic dive, and resurfaced with seaweed in his hair and dignity dripping. Emily exclaimed, "Oh my God", with the cadence of someone still learning Spanish, and everyone laughed until their stomachs hurt. Through tears of laughter, Migue offered her a shell as a trophy; she accepted it with the solemnity of someone who collects moments.

The beach became a board of voices. Luis and his steel band mixed with the **pleneros** of the barrio, vendors walked by with frituras, and children ran in every direction. Lula and Emily let themselves be carried by the music; the steps did not matter, only the synchrony of two teenagers learning to call each other friends. Sergio attempted salsa moves he had seen in videos and created a choreography made of effort and good intentions; Dani clapped like someone cheering from the stands.

When the adults arrived, the party truly began. They ate as if they had not eaten in days: **mofongo** that smelled like home, fried fish, **tostones** that crunched, and **empanadillas** that filled the mouth with memory. Emily tried everything with curiosity, saying in a blend of English and Spanish, "It is like party food, and home." Her honest laughter opened new windows in the conversation.

When night came, the coast changed its attire. The bonfires began to glow like a necklace of lights along the shore. People gathered with candles and small offerings. Tradition called for waiting until midnight to jump the wave and leave wishes in the water. Some murmured superstitions, wetting the back of the neck for good luck, staring at the moon without blinking to attract love, and the mixture of faith and playfulness spread among everyone.

The teenagers entertained themselves with bets about who would feel the coldest or who would be the bravest. At midnight they held hands and made a collective jump, a splash that was not a holy ritual but the leap of joy. The water bit for a second, and their voices blended into a brief chorus that lasted as long as the foam. They handed out superstitions as if they were shells, promises to return, wishes wrapped in salt.

At the end, sitting on the shore, they let grains of sand fall from their hands as if offering tiny pieces of the future. Emily, now less foreign and more friend, whispered in Spanish with her distant accent, "This place is magic. Thank you." Dani smiled knowingly; he understood he had shared something that did not appear in any exchange-student brochure. Migue reminded her of the hero's shell. She put it in her bag like someone placing away a small treasure.

As dawn approached, the group began to say goodbye with salty hugs and promises to return. Emily and Dani walked toward the parking lot, sandals in hand and hair still wet. Before disappearing among the walkway lights, Emily turned around and with her American accent shouted, laughing:

"The Poza is not for sale! The beaches belong to the people!"

The voices dissolved into the warm air, mixing with the sound of the sea and the echo of a summer that did not want to leave.

On the ride back, laughter clung to them, sand stayed in their pockets, and promises were made under their breath. Under the moonlight they felt closer to the sea and farther from the urgency of growing up. La Poza del Obispo kept their footprints and returned to them a simple truth: some days, because of how they are shared, become memory.

CHAPTER 16
BUSES, TALES AND MILES

Our life was full of adventures. But of all those adventures, the very best was going to town. Going to town was where you learned to dream about "other things." You put on clean shorts and a fresh shirt because you could not show up in town looking all "tó tirao." You stood at some corner of the barrio, on the main road, waiting for a *carro público* or the bus.

The *guagua* was more than transportation. It was a rolling stage of Puerto Rican life. Inside it fit students with backpacks full of dreams, workers with tired hands, older women with their market bags, and couples who brushed fingertips as they paid the fare. The driver was the DJ of the highway and, sometimes, the barrio therapist. The smell of sweat mixed with the scent of *bacalaítos* wrapped in napkins, and the echo of conversations created a symphony only those who rode the bus could understand. When the *guagua* took off with that old but steady roar, it felt like it was telling us that even if the road was long and full of curves, we were all in it together, sharing destination, laughter and memories under the same Caribbean sun.

The other option was the *carro público*. And in my town, taking a *carro público* was almost a mystical experience. You never knew if you were actually going to reach your destination or come home with a brand-new story to tell. If you were lucky, you sat in the front. If it was full, you squeezed in the back like a canned sardine.

Sometimes the driver would stop and announce,

"I have space for one." Half begging for an adult to get in so he could complete the fare.

"Fine, I will carry him on my lap," the grandmother would say, holding a wrinkled bill.

And just like that, you ended up sitting on your grandmother's lap, miserable and defeated.

If you got the window seat, you stuck your hand out to feel the breeze. Inside the car, the air conditioning was pure imagination, because it did not exist. Everyone fanned themselves with whatever they had: a newspaper, a notebook, even a sandal. If traffic hit, it turned into a party. Someone pulled out a pack of crackers, another shared a juice, while the driver lowered the radio volume. As the grown-ups talked about the latest barrio gossip, you felt the wind sliding through your fingers and pretended you were on a roller coaster. Sometimes you fell asleep and only heard the old folks complaining in the distance.

A *carro público* cost fifteen cents from my barrio to town. Being so poor, that was a small fortune, and sometimes we preferred walking rather than giving up those fifteen cents we could use on the pinball machine.

The creativity of *carro público* drivers was unmatched. And nothing was more versatile than that damn metal box that managed to fit an impossible amount of people. The chubbier ones sat in the front, everyone else squeezed in the back. If you were too large, you better "fleet" the entire ride, renting the car Uber-style. On the best days, you ended up between two gorgeous *mamisongas*. On the worst days, you were trapped between two grumpy elders with a smell straight from hell.

And the waiting... what torture when the car was one passenger short, and that last person refused to appear. That car was not moving until every seat was full. The driver did not care if you were dehydrating inside, he stayed outside in the shade until his sardine can was packed. Nobody was willing to throw in an extra fifteen cents to cover the missing passenger. Six full fares in the back seat, no weight limit, kids and smelly infants not included. Sometimes you returned to the barrio with numb feet, cramped legs and your little family jewels so squashed you could barely climb out of that cursed metal coffin.

And then there were the social classes. In our world everything was solved with nicknames: the poor, the very poor, the **cafres**, and those **come gofio** that seemed like a species of their own. The amazing thing was that once everyone settled in, at least for a moment, class differences disappeared. No more office workers, nurses, housewives, teachers or students. The only difference inside the car was the opinion war between the *Penepés* and the *Populares*.

The driver only had to say, "This country is messed up," and boom, World War III began. They argued about the hospital with no medicine, statehood, supermarket prices, crime, drugs, and of course everything was the fault of the party in power.

"Hurry up, Pancho," the teacher would say, the most sensible and educated of the group, "these people need to get off before they kill each other." You could hear the Pentecostals rebuking the devil. But inside that car there was one untouchable saint: Luis Muñoz Marín. After all the shouting, the laughter served as a cease-fire, and everyone said, "See you tomorrow," eager to repeat the whole show again.

Maybe that is why there were fewer crazies back then. People got home relaxed. That sardine can was their de-stresser, their Zoloft, their free therapy session.

Politicians should be forced to ride in *carros públicos*. Maybe then, they would understand what it feels like to live in the skin of the people, instead of speaking from so high above. And when it comes to *cafres* and *come gofio*, may the devil take a number and collect them all together.

That was the *carro público* of my homeland, loud, hot, unpredictable and full of life. In every ride there was a joke, a song, a lesson in patience and a reminder that in my country, even a traffic jam can be a reason to smile.

CHAPTER 17
THE ROOSTER PIT

The 681 road was more than a strip of asphalt, it was the thread that stitched our lives between the barrio and the town. It curved along the coast, with the salty wind tapping the car windows and the sound of the waves keeping rhythm with every turn. It was a narrow ribbon that separated El Islote from the rest of the island, yet the same one that kept us connected to the world. To cross it, you had to pass the Puente del Vigía, that old guardian of iron and cement standing watch over the channel, as if deciding who entered and who left. Every time we crossed, it felt like we were leaving behind the calm of the barrio and stepping into the bustle of town life.

Along the road, the fritura stands peeked out from the shoulder, releasing the irresistible smell of bacalaítos, alcapurrias and pastellilos. Between one fritura and the next were the produce and **quenepa** stands, run by weathered hands and wide smiles. Sometimes the vendors knew you by name, and the greeting was guaranteed: "Look who's coming, Doña Geno's grandson!" Farther down, the mangroves spread out like a green labyrinth where blue crabs ran to hide. It was common to see the boys knee-deep in mud with a rope and a bucket, hunting for their next dinner or simply killing time with jokes and mischief.

And when you reached La Gallera, you knew the final stretch was close. But that place was beautiful chaos: no parking whatsoever, so cars lined the road bumper to bumper. On Sundays it turned into a cheerful traffic jam, a full-blown pueblo **tapón**, where people lowered their windows to greet each other, share a drink, or debate which rooster had the most fire in him. Road 681 pulsed with life, music, voices, and that human warmth only our little corner of the world could give.

The gallera is not as rowdy as it used to be, but every Sunday it still opens its doors, like someone who refuses to let a tradition die. The tin roof has more patches than an old pair of pants, and the faded sign that reads "Gallera El Pasaje" is barely visible through the rust and peeling paint.

Inside Don Severo reigned, the same old gallero as always. With his hat tilted, towel over his shoulder and that midday-sun smile, he walked slowly between the cages, greeting everyone like he was the mayor. He insisted the gallera was not dead, only "resting with its eyes open." And even though the crowds were smaller than in the glory days, all it took was someone shouting, "¡Van los gallos!" for the old friends to come shuffling in, dragging their flip-flops and their memories.

The air smelled of Palo Viejo rum and Cuban cigars. From her little booth, Doña Tomasa sold pastelillos and alcapurrias with the pride of someone running a five-star restaurant. She liked to joke that her frying pan had seen more drama than the pit itself.

One Sunday, a scene unfolded that still makes the whole barrio laugh. Chuíto brought his new rooster, The Immortal. He had spent weeks bragging about it, swearing that not even a hurricane could knock him down. But when they released him in the ring, the poor rooster got distracted by a piece of bread someone had dropped... and instead of charging at his rival, he ran straight to peck at the bread.

The crowd erupted in laughter, and Chuíto, red as a hot pepper, yelled,

"It's not hunger, it's strategy! He's calculating the perfect moment!"

Seconds later, The Immortal was sprinting away from the other rooster... with the bread in his beak. From that day on, nobody in the barrio called him Chuíto again. He became forever known as Señor Pan.

Still, every Sunday the same faces returned. Some came for the thrill, others for nostalgia, and others just to chat. Among the old planks, the shouts of "Hit him!" and the clinking of beer bottles, you could feel the gallera still beating, even if a little slower.

When the sun dipped behind the mango tree, Don Severo always closed with the same words,

"Times change, yes... but as long as someone comes, the gallera lives."

CHAPTER 18
DOWNTOWN
PUERTO RICO

E very child arrives in town holding the hand of someone who loves them. In our case, it was our grandmother's firm hand, squeezing as if the town were too big to trust a loose little boy on his own.

Arriving in town felt like crossing an invisible border. You left the barrio as a child and stepped into the town feeling almost like a tourist, even if you carried no luggage. You were always held by your grandmother's firm hand, that hand that knew more roads than any map and squeezed just enough to warn you without speaking. In town they did not let go of you because, as she said, "someone might snatch you," and you nodded even if you did not really understand who you were supposed to fear. The crowd moved like a restless river around you, and you floated inside it wide-eyed, watching colors, voices, and stories rush by. Every corner seemed to whisper a new possibility. In that bustling world of taxis, pigeons, perfume, sweat, and sun, a child could learn what it meant to dream beyond the barrio. Still, between her warm hand and the town's hum that seemed to sing in your ear, you learned early that life had two heartbeats: the barrio's, which rocked you gently, and the town's, which woke you up.

With that steady grip and your heart skipping a beat, you entered the town as if stepping onto a lit-up stage. And that was how the adventure always began.

Town had its own heartbeat. People poured into the streets until the crowd became a living tide. It was a symphony of children laughing and crying, men flinging piropos like confetti, women walking with the grace of queens under the Caribbean sun, eccentrics drifting through their private universes, and the unmistakable click of secretaries' heels on sunbaked sidewalks. At times the crowd felt so large it swallowed you whole, and you drifted through it half-visible, half-forgotten. You waited at stoplights while pigeons fought over crumbs at your feet, and by mid-morning the humidity slid down your back like a warm hand. You chased the shade as if it were treasure.

You walked with your eyes wide open, absorbing everything. The storefronts. The shoe displays in La Gloria that sparkled like unattainable dreams. The adults nudged you to keep moving, but wonder slowed your steps. At the next intersection another wave of sound and color stole your attention. Passing the Rivera Biascochea Travel Agency, you imagined boarding an airplane or sailing away on a cruise ship to somewhere with cold winds and strange languages. Another nudge brought you back to reality, reminding you that dreams had their place, but town had a schedule.

Your senses tangled with the smells drifting through the streets, pizza from Mi Casita, the earthy scent of vegetables at the Plaza del Mercado, the sweet perfume of fresh bread from Panadería La Estrella. People rushed past so quickly their glances skimmed over you like water over stone. Town was full of so many precious things to look at that you could not settle your gaze on any single one.

The town eccentrics frightened you at first, yet they were part of the landscape. No one knew how they got there, since nadie quería darles pon. You turned one corner and there stood Pilichi. Another, and there was Paquita el Congo. Then La Machaca, Calu, Colega, Luis Sopanda, Juan Ardilla, Coco Seco. The wandering angels of the pueblo. They walked all day, greeting everyone, pausing in corners as if waiting for secrets to arrive, making gestures only the wind understood. They collected cans, carried bags, pushed shopping carts that rattled like percussion. Over time they became folklore, stories whispered from balcony to balcony.

There was also the man whose answer to everything was "Que se joda (screw it)." And truth be told, some days life answered with that same philosophy.

After a while, the people in town all looked a little peculiar, especially those who walked without hurry or direction. In town, nobody needed to cling too tightly to sanity. We all drifted a bit, dazzled by the mannequins posed like silent divas behind department store glass.

In Luis Muñoz Rivera Plaza the old men played dominoes with the seriousness of philosophers and the pride of kings.The plaza was the soul of town, a crossroads where every barrio converged. Públicos idled along the curb. Ice cream vendors rang their bells. Artisans laid out their creations. Pigeons strutted like small, arrogant landlords. Couples who never dared kiss in their own barrio's plaza kissed boldly here, where anonymity was a blanket. Children splashed in the fountain, chasing drops of sunlight. Carnival lit the plaza in season, and the music stage rose each year like a promise. History lingered there too, in the Casa Alcaldía, its walls holding stories of rebellions and long-forgotten nights.

Passing the Oliver Theater, the scent of popcorn curled into your hunger. A little farther ahead your grandmother bought you a meat empanadilla and a grape Old Colony from a chinchorro, the kind of treat that tasted like pure childhood.

The small shops tucked into narrow streets were town's hidden treasure chests. They were the stores of affection, the "I will write it down for you" stores, the "come tomorrow and I will save one" stores. That was where your grandmother bought fabric, buttons, pots, candles, rope, copper cups, hats, and all the humble things the bigger stores never bothered with. In that string of tiny shops, you could find everything your house, your stomach, or your imagination needed.

And no visit was complete without a stop at the pharmacy to buy Alcoholado Superior 70 and Vicks VapoRub, the sacred remedies your grandmother trusted as if blessed by saints.

CHAPTER 19
THE LITTLE JAR THAT CURES EVERYTHING

J ust like in my grandmother's house, in Doña
Pura's home there was no doctor or pharmacy
that could compete. For her, the cure for everything lived inside that little blue jar of VapoRub.

One time her grandson showed up with a
toothache.

"Grandma, it hurts right here..."

Without hesitation, Doña Pura smeared VapoRub
on his cheek.

"That will numb it, mijo."

Another day her son-in-law complained about back
pain.

"Rub some VapoRub on it and give him a good
massage, that pulls everything out."

The neighbor arrived with Zika and even had a

fever. And what did Doña Pura do? She rubbed VapoRub on her temples, on her chest, and even behind her ears.

"With this you sweat the sickness out."

But the best story was when the refrigerator broke, and the food started to smell strange. Doña Pura, very serious, opened the jar and put it inside.

"So the bad smell goes away."

The kids in the neighborhood swore that if someone broke an arm, Doña Pura would never take them to the hospital.

"Bring me the VapoRub, that sticks it back together."

Everyone knew that little jar did not cure everything, but one thing was true. Doña Pura gave a kind of affection that healed more than any medicine.

In the Puerto Rican household medicine cabinet, there are two patron saints of home remedies, Alcoholado Superior 70 and Vicks VapoRub. She, the Alcoholado, always ready, strong, fierce, with that smell powerful enough to wake the dead. He, the VapoRub, softer but just as miraculous, with that menthol that opens both the chest and the soul.

In the old houses they sat together on the shelf like a lifelong married couple. When one could not do the job, the other took over. If you got a massage with Alcoholado, you ended up anointed with VapoRub "just in case." If anything hurt, together they gave you a full healing ceremony.

It was the unbeatable formula, a blend of science, faith, and cariño. If the Alcoholado was the spark that awakened your senses, the VapoRub was the hug that calmed them. Together they were the perfect pair, one stung and the other comforted.

If Puerto Rico had a national medical coat of arms, instead of a snake it would have a bottle of Alcoholado and a jar of VapoRub crossed like swords of well-being.

So never forget, Cough at night, fever during the day, Alcoholado and VapoRub, and joy comes your way.

CHAPTER 20
THE MARKETPLACE

Visiting the market was an adventure all its own, a kind of street carnival made of colors, voices, and smells. A shiver of excitement ran through you the moment you heard the cacophony of shouts coming from every direction. Vendors called out their offers at the top of their lungs to draw in customers, and those customers bargained back with equal determination. The constant rumble of voices gave life to that enormous, shadowy building. At times you felt almost claustrophobic in the powerful tide of strangers who always seemed to be in a hurry.

But Abuela knew the place by heart. She walked fast, and you had to trot beside her to keep from being trampled. Someone always bumped you with a bag full of produce or brushed past you without noticing. And everywhere you looked, things you had imagined and things you had never dreamed of owning were laid out for sale.

The old men of the plaza seemed to know Abuela. You noticed how she exchanged short greetings with the vendors, old friends catching up. She would whisper, "That one was my childhood neighbor, that lady sewed my dresses, that other man was your grandfather's compadre." Before long, they were greeting you too, as if the market itself had adopted you.

Before you reached the next stall, every fiber of your being buzzed with anticipation. There was always a vendor offering you something to taste. Your mouth watered the moment you saw a table full of ham slices or trays of dulces. An old man would hand you a piece of cantaloupe so sweet that the juice ran down your wrist like honey. Abuela made you stop at each stand to touch the products, to feel their textures, to learn to choose well. She placed coins in your palm so you could pay and practice taking your change. You hopped from stall to stall until you memorized them all, your arms filling with so many bags that you could barely carry them.

Mountains of orange mangos piled high, bunches of green plantains hanging like chandeliers, golden pineapples shining like tropical crowns. Vegetables for caldo, cilantro, recao, tomatoes, avocados. In every row there was a specialty: sacks of nuts and dried fruits, mounds of powdered spices stacked by color, bags of beans, flour, cheeses, eggs, and sweets. Aromas rose from every corner, rich and unfamiliar, wrapping around your senses until you could taste them in the air. Some made you cough just by smelling them.

After so many bags, so many lessons in agronomy and mathematics, you reached the last stall exhausted and starving. You could think of nothing but food. Abuela kept chatting, but all you could picture was a sugar-coated doughnut that would calm the beast in your stomach. The desire was so strong you could already taste it. You pleaded with Abuela, and once she finally agreed, you hurried her along, but the more you rushed her, the slower she walked. She too was tired, nearly dragging the heavy bags that knocked against her legs.

And yet, when you finally stepped out of the market, sweaty and worn but filled with delight, you knew you wanted to come back.

Because the market did that to you. It pulled you in, shook you awake, and handed you back to the street a little richer, not in coins, but in stories.

We left the market tired but happy, our hands sweaty from carrying so many bags and our clothes clinging to the smells of fruit, spices, and people. We walked out sticky, rumpled, dragging our feet a little, yet somehow lighter than when we arrived. Now we understand why. The market gave us memories louder than the shouting vendors, sweeter than the melon samples, and stronger than the scent of sofrito that clung to our shirts. In that maze of voices and paper bags, we learned that childhood is built from small moments that later become treasures, and that every errand with our grandmother was, quietly and without ceremony, an act of love. Between the vendors calling out their prices and the rustle of bags brushing against our legs, our island whispered a truth we have carried ever since: joy lives in the ordinary, and memory is the homeland we take with us wherever we go.

CHAPTER 21
WHEN CREDIT WAS A HANDSHAKE

C redit and trust walked hand in hand, and in those days they were essential. Poor families were big, but money was scarce. So, people survived by "cogiendo fiao," buying on credit.

Out in the barrios, in the little corner stores of the poor, that whole credit system was invented. There were no plastic cards, no microchips. All that existed was "your word," because every sale was face to face, and a poor person's word was the most valuable thing they owned. In the barrio you did not just get credit at Don Toño's store, you also got credit from the barber, the hairdresser, and even the espiritista. With time people sold everything, and where everything was sold, everything could be bought on credit, washing machines, fans, televisions, socks, even underwear. That was how the poor managed, and how the small merchants survived.

At Don Toño's colmado you did your shopping, they handed you your goods, and you walked home without paying a cent. Abuela would say, "Go to Don Toño's store and give him this list, tell him to write it down." That was enough to come back with a little bag of groceries. In a big notebook, with a small pencil tied to it with a string, Don Toño wrote down whatever you took on credit. At the end of the month, you paid it, and then you borrowed again.

And that was when the Arabs took advantage of the system. The *quincalleros* par excellence. Every week they would drive through in a white van announcing their "cholchás," cheap goods and bargains, cloth, bedsheets, costume jewelry, combs, buttons, pocket mirrors, bracelets, pillows, rugs. They traveled with suitcases full of merchandise and sold door to door. Once you stopped them to look, they pulled out a catalog with lamps, furniture, even perfume. By the end you had bought a whole bedroom set.

People in the countryside and in the distant barrios, those who did not have access to town, waited for them because through them they could buy small decorations and little luxuries they would not find anywhere else. Many times, they gave you credit too, wrote it all down in a notebook, and you paid little by little. They brought with them a tiny piece of another world that slipped into the humblest jíbaro homes.

But, as in every flock, there was always a black sheep. Some never paid a cent. They had no money for their debts, yet somehow always had enough for a bottle. Others brought a tiny **"abonito,"** a peace offering that barely scratched the balance. Little by little they sowed mistrust, and the merchants, tired of chasing ghosts, harvested caution. Before long a familiar sign appeared behind every counter, written in bold letters: **"Hoy no fío, mañana sí"** (Today I do not give credit, tomorrow I will). It hung there like a joke everyone understood. And even though Don Toño might not have been giving credit "today," the truth was that his heart stayed open, just like the door of his little colmado, from sunrise to sunset.

CHAPTER 22

LOVE BORINQUEÑA STYLE

There he was, perched on that mountainside, swallowed whole by discouragement. He knew he had no one to blame but himself, yet stubbornness pushed him to fault the whole world except the man in the mirror. For months he had searched for work, leaving the house with his résumé tucked into a worn folder under his arm, knocking on doors, filling out applications. But the answer was always the same, "We will call you," and they never did. Hope dimmed little by little, and frustration began to settle into his bones like cold.

At home, sadness disguised itself as anger.

"Arroz con habichuelas again?" he would complain, sour and irritated.

Any small detail became a spark: a shirt folded the wrong way, a sigh taken the wrong way. He raised his voice, argued over nonsense, threw out complaints that meant nothing except in the heart of his little wife. But deep down it was not against her. It was against himself, against the helplessness of not being able to provide, against the shadow of failure that followed him everywhere. She knew it, and although it hurt, she endured those little fights with patience, because she understood that beneath the anger there was a wounded man who still dreamed of rising again.

Women always know. I dare say that most of the time they are deeply spiritual and divinely inspired. There is no doubt that the Divine created woman and man, but we were tuned to different frequencies.

Marusha did not let anyone intimidate her. She could easily dress herself in the fierceness of a lioness, but she preferred the gentleness of a dove. That little Boricua knew how to smile even when she felt like screaming inside.

And running out the door was the only way he ever came out victorious from their arguments. All their quarrels followed the same pattern. If it was not about the coffee being too light, it was a towel hung in the wrong place. If it was not about the food, it was the ironing. He would storm out of the house like a soul chased by the devil, furious, fuming, waving his hands without daring to shout, punching at the air, biting his lips, because he knew that in that house he did not even have the freedom to raise his voice and walk out yelling. His little wife stayed behind, sending him a thousand blessings, silently asking the Divine to calm her husband's temper and keep him from having a bad moment.

That is how Puerto Rican women are. They are hurricane and breeze. They are a song born from sea and mountain. They carry the fire of the sun on their skin and the tenderness of rain in their soul. They are mystery, clarity, fire, and dew. Their voice can be sweet, yet also thunder when it needs to be. When they ask God to watch over you, it is because they would rather be the ones doing it. It is not that they are submissive, it is that when they love, they love with their whole heart. They are like the ceiba after the storm, rising again a thousand times. Their hearts are embroidered with salt and sugar. They are faithful because they are thinking of you at every hour.

Boricua women are tender and affectionate, and you know they love you because their heart opens and, from a distance, you can almost hear their heartbeat.

When they look into your eyes, their own eyes shine. The Puerto Rican woman is a living volcano, burning you with her passion. When you fall in love with one, every time you say her name you sing a song, she inspires love poems, and she spills joy into your life. With a woman like this, living in anger is impossible.

CHAPTER 23
THE HEAT OF DESIRE

I n search of something better, a goodbye always feels necessary, or perhaps inevitable. Shortly before his departure, the family prepared a great farewell for him, a "see you later" mixed with tears and hope.

Early that morning Doña María and Marusha were already up washing, chopping, peeling, and massaging the vegetables. "We have to grind the meat, we have to peel the potatoes," said Doña María from inside that humble kitchen that looked like a rainbow decorated with fruits and root vegetables. On a table covered with a plastic cloth there were green peppers, red bell peppers, tamarind, lemons, oranges, and grapefruits. In a little corner sat the ají peppers, celery, and onions.

For Puerto Ricans there is no food in the world as

delicious as our own. Our flavors carry a rustic, countryside soul that we call Criollo. Puerto Rican cuisine is a blend of cultures mixed together by the noble spirit of the Taíno, the conquistador spirit of the Spaniards, the strength of the enslaved Africans, the adventurous spirit of the Danes, the revolutionary spirit of the French, the philosophical spirit of the Chinese, and the competitive spirit of the Italians. From all that came a cocktail of flavors that reaches far beyond the limits of our island. For ordinary days we have the perfect marriage, white rice, red or pink beans, and a small piece of meat. But for special occasions, that is when you throw the door out the window, the food must be good and abundant. That is when a recipe is born that can feed an entire neighborhood.

Doña María pulled out the big pot she kept hidden under the sink, the one reserved for serious cooking, and filled it with yams, yautía, malanga, and green bananas to boil until they softened like memory. On a wide table, arranged on bamboo plates, lay the kingdom of flavors: beans, anise, saffron, cilantro, cumin, annatto, ginger, bay leaves, oregano, mint, almonds, parsley, and peppers in every shade the island sun could invent. In campesino cooking every herb has purpose, there is no such thing as a useless one. The leaves are never simply cut, they are crushed and ground so their fragrance can run free. Waiting in a glass jar was the sofrito, prepared the night before with recao, cilantrillo, onions, sweet peppers, ajíes, and garlic, all pounded in a wooden pilón with a touch of oil to give the rice its perfect island color.

On the stove there was a giant caldero for the arroz con gandules. In one corner of the kitchen sat a can of lard and another of oil. Meanwhile Don Pedro went to his small plot of land to cut a few bananas leaves to wrap the **pasteles** and to pull down a few avocados from the tree, which was heavy with fruit. Behind the house he grabbed a long pole that he used to knock down the breadfruit that grew high in the tall tree.

Inside that apparent chaos there was a very organized disorganization. One washed, chopped, and peeled. The second crushed, massaged, and ground. The third strained, boiled, flipped, and added. In the mother-in-law's house there were no written recipes, everything was judged "by eye." She knew by taste, by smell, by color. Her daughter seemed to have inherited the culinary art straight through the bloodline. They knew when the broth was perfect because they dipped in a finger to test the temperature. If they liked it, everyone would love it. The whole neighborhood was invited to the feast through the aromas escaping from the kitchen windows. The cooks never knew how many guests would show up, they cooked for the whole neighborhood, just in case.

There was a quiet sensuality in the kitchen when you watched your partner dip a finger into the ladle, taste the seasoning, and smile at the flavor lingering there. It stirred a flutter in your stomach. Marusha cooked with a kind of slow-burning passion, awakening an appetite that went far beyond anything simmering in the pots. Some foods, with their curves and colors, seemed made to inspire the imagination, turning into gentle provocations. The aromas, warm and familiar, rose like an embrace, awakening every sense, a small feast of longing and tenderness.

Noticing that he could not take his eyes off her, his wife lifted the ladle and offered him a taste, inviting him with a playful glance to dip his finger and try the broth. In that moment her simple house dress seemed to transform, moving with the breeze like the gown of a Greek goddess, light as palm leaves swaying at dusk. A familiar warmth stirred in him. There was an almost sacred pleasure in kissing those lips of hers, a sweetness that felt crafted by divine hands. Few things were richer than savoring affection slowly, letting it bloom like a flavor on the tongue. A sudden craving washed over him, not for food alone, but for closeness, for the comfort of being wanted. A quiet heat rose through him, soft but insistent, like the first spark under the pot before it turns into a rolling boil.

In his imagination he lifted his wife's apron as if it were the only garment she wore. He longed to taste her, to draw her close, to savor the warmth of that cinnamon skin that tempted him without effort. Her lips, full and red like a slice of fresh papaya, awakened a hunger that had nothing to do with the food simmering on the stove. He imagined warming his hands with butter and gliding them along her waist, following the rhythm of bomba and plena that lived in her hips. He wanted to lose himself in her embrace, sweet as cane rum, and taste the trace of coquito that seemed to rest at her navel like a secret offering.

Marusha must have been made with great tenderness. Her fair skin was soft as rose petals, her eyes carried a quiet kindness, and her lips held the color of tropical fruit at its ripest. Her body, graceful and confident, invited affection without demanding it. A single mischievous glance from her could send a whole message without a word. Her hips swayed like palm fronds dancing to the ocean breeze.

She was a woman firmly rooted, guided by a heart that felt deeply and a spirit that seemed touched by the divine. Marusha made him feel loved and wanted and seen. In intimacy she was natural, open, and unafraid of pleasure. It only took a few seconds of shared gaze, a smile from her to him, and he would fall under her spell again. In private she was bold, tender, and full of fire, a warm Caribbean storm, and he was a man who lived to be invited into that whirlwind and to surrender, without resistance, to the passion they created together.

Who would not feel a hunger of another kind before such a sight. He watched her with a tenderness so deep it felt like a secret he could barely hold. His desire was obvious even to himself, yet Marusha followed her rhythm in the kitchen, softening a tortilla in her hands as if nothing unusual were unfolding in the air. He simmered like the pot on the stove, first on low heat, then medium, until emotion rose in him the way broth does when it reaches a gentle boil. He longed for the sweetness of her kisses, for the warmth that always met him when she leaned close. He imagined standing behind her, arms around her waist, his heartbeat resting against her back. The curve of her neck carried scents that betrayed him, a mix of vanilla and ripe fruit, her hair smelled faintly of strawberries, and the warmth of her skin held the soft sweetness of home.The most delicious food is meant to be savored, not rushed. Love is the same. You must arrive gently, a little unhurried, the wine is the playful words that intoxicate you with sighs. There is no clock or time when you are lost among fruit trees.

A sudden shout from a neighbor snapped him out of his trance, "Man, move out of the way, find somewhere else to stand." The lovers laughed, knowing that the best part of that feast would be tasted later at night, under the glow of fireflies and without witnesses. Waking from that enchantment was the only bitter flavor he had tasted. To cool his desire and recover his senses he stepped out into the yard, his knees still trembling.

CHAPTER 24
GOODBYES ARE ALWAYS SAD

It was the day of his departure. The moment he knew would come sooner or later, yet he feared it with every corner of his heart. He had to say goodbye to the people who mattered most, the ones who filled his life with meaning. But how does a person say goodbye without feeling that something inside has been torn away? He needed them, because without them he felt like nobody. It was as if an elephant had settled on his chest, squeezing the breath out of him, leaving behind a hollow space so deep it felt like a black hole. He knew he would only feel whole again when he had them back at his side. He tried not to cry... but tears do not listen to reason.

It was time to leave, maybe for good. What was happening inside him was difficult and painful, almost unbearable. He knew this was one of those moments when he had to protect her, protect her heart and his own. They both knew their love would hold them together despite the distance, that they only needed to reach for each other in their minds to feel the warmth again. But in the moment of departure, sacrifice becomes the toll you pay. And even though it hurt, he loved her more in that instant than he ever had. This long, painful goodbye was proof of that love.

His heart felt a blade running straight through it. Leaving was not easy. It was not a final goodbye, but it wounded as if it were. They held each other tightly and, as he walked down the rocky slope toward the car that would take him to the airport, he looked back wishing all of this were a bad dream. But it wasn't. It was real, painfully real. All he could do was bury the ache now and promise himself he would face it later.

He felt as if he had lost a piece of himself, and the weight in his chest was impossible to explain. That day, they looked at each other with their souls uncovered. She asked him to take care of himself and whispered an "I love you" soft enough to break him in two. "Please be safe... come back to me," she said, blowing him a kiss as the car began to pull away. Their tired, tear-blurred eyes searched for each other one last time, as if trying to memorize every line of a face that distance might steal from them.

They said goodbye without saying the word, as if silence itself could hold them tighter than language ever could. He wanted to speak, to say something that would seal the moment forever, but no words came. The tears had their own language, and the heart... the heart had its own way of letting go.

CHAPTER 25
UNDER THE BIG CITY LIGHTS

E very ending carries a new beginning inside it, something special that grows into a new life. But a new life does not arrive wrapped like a gift, with pretty ribbons or mariachi music welcoming you. When a new life begins, there is always insecurity and uncertainty. A new life is an adventure, and to walk it you need a brave heart and steady feet.

A new beginning is the strangest thing, because it feels as if everything that happened before, every joy and mistake and memory, was only the prequel to what comes next. It is like finishing a chapter in a book and starting a new one without knowing anything about the story. This new chapter moves slower, as if every day hands you only one word at a time. So all you can do is keep your eyes on the horizon and your mind tuned in, like a newborn learning one small step at a time.

He arrived in an unfamiliar place. A big city where the streets seemed more crowded, the people less friendly, and everyone focused only on themselves. A city that never slept. A train that groaned like an old saxophone. A wind that combed through the skyscrapers as if challenging them to stand tall. Nobody cared if you were cold or if you were lost. He walked looking at the ground, the same way everyone else walked, because no one seemed to notice anyone's existence. He felt invisible in the middle of so many people.

It was a city of wide avenues, skyscrapers, stadiums and theaters, ice rinks and baseball fields. Churches, mosques, temples, enormous bridges, and underground trains. Hospitals, libraries, police stations, prisons, and busy streets full of people. The city was divided between wealth and poverty. Downtown had luxury stores with giant windows and bright signs. The poor neighborhoods were filled with hardship, graffiti on the walls, and the "perfume" of car exhaust, factory smoke, and sewer fumes.

In the morning the city was a maze of noisy streets and alleys. You could hear the honking before the sun came up. Impatient drivers tried to reach their offices, arguing with bus drivers and mothers dropping off their kids. Long lines formed at the bakery. Construction workers filled the streets in their neon jackets, and street sweepers and garbage collectors worked while everyone else ate breakfast. Executives and professionals crammed into the buses. By mid-morning, when the rush had disappeared and people had reached their destinations, the cars vanished into dark parking garages like caves. The city woke slowly but firmly, bringing with it new opportunities, work, school projects, science assignments, math homework, plenty of coffee, and bagels. For many people a new day carried a small spark of hope.

He took the bus at dawn when everyone on board looked half-asleep, their reactions slow. Some read the newspaper, others meditated, others simply held on so they would not fall. The bus was full. Black and white, Latino, Asian, European, every nationality represented. Tall, short, thin, heavy, each person a little universe of their own. With time you came to recognize them, even knowing exactly where each one would get off.

The first time he went up a skyscraper was on a summer night. What he saw took his breath away. He felt a little dizzy when he leaned close to the window.

In the distance the streets shimmered with lights, as if someone had thrown a handful of glitter as far as the eye could see. It was too dark to distinguish individual buildings, but the lights were a whole spectacle, and the cars looked like little ants with red dots. All he could do was sigh.

At night there were lights everywhere, from cars, restaurants, and stores that ran twenty-four hours a day. Sounds changed after dark. Fire truck sirens, ambulances, and police cars warned you it was time to be indoors. Night fell early. You heard the click of the streetlamps turning on, but you could not see the stars. The sky shifted from gray to black. You did not want to be outside unless you had a good reason. These were hours to reset and "recharge your batteries." The only smiles came from bars and restaurants where people talked and relaxed after a long day. People walked faster, with their hands in their pockets. Maybe that was why you rarely felt a firm handshake. He always thought it was because they were cold, or maybe like Pedro Navaja, they hid a knife for protection. The glow of the moon was never enough to light the darkness.

Nighttime was the hardest. Loneliness swallowed him, and he felt that the only heart beating in the apartment was his own. For the first time in his life he felt truly alone. When you miss the people you love, it feels like something pinches your heart and tightens it to give you more pain. You wake up alone, eat breakfast alone, lunch alone, dinner alone, listen to music alone. You ride the bus alone and walk home alone. In this new life, loneliness was the only friend he could trust.

CHAPTER 26
IN THE ARMS OF WINTER

The first time he saw snow he was stunned into silence. The sky gathered silver and charcoal clouds that looked ready to empty their secrets over the city. When those feathered crystals finally began to fall, it felt as if the Divine were scattering glitter over the metropolis. The snow was far more beautiful than anything he had imagined, and a first snowfall is like a first love, something you carry forever.

The streets wrapped themselves in white, and the trees glowed with a beauty straight out of a Christmas card. He stepped outside because he needed to touch it. The cold had not yet settled in, and the flakes landed on his face as he blinked, tiny specks of frost settling on his skin. The snow tickled his eyelashes. Each flake felt as if it were meant for his hands. He removed his gloves and let them rest on his fingers, lifting them to his mouth as if tasting a secret.

Seeing snow fall for the first time is a moment of pure happiness. The excitement is real. It is one of those simple moments in life that can only be lived, not explained. The world becomes a giant snow globe, the kind children shake just to watch the flakes swirl in invisible currents. Fresh snow on the sidewalks reminded him of beach sand, and stepping on it gave him the urge to be the first one to leave footprints, to create the path himself.

And while adults think mostly about the beauty and romance of snow, a good snowfall means something very different to the young. It means battle. The more snow, the better. The excitement of a snowball fight is impossible to resist. As soon as a few snowballs were formed and stacked, the first round began, the first of many. Snowball fights are wars, and wars are meant to be won.

It never took long before someone decided it was time to build a snowman. You rolled three enormous balls of snow, shaping them until the abominable little creature took form. Some became true masterpieces. A long carrot for a nose, two buttons for eyes, and a pair of branches for arms. Proudly you admired it, praying it would survive a few days before melting away.

When the joy of snow began to fade, your lips turned blue, and your fingers stiffened. That was when you discovered that behind all the beauty, snow had its darker side. Shoveling became work, a kind of cold-weather punishment. All over the neighborhood you heard the scrape of metal shovels carving paths through sidewalks and driveways. Sometimes you were not even done shoveling when a second snowfall arrived. The wind grew fierce and slapped your face raw. You lowered your head until your chin touched your chest. Your feet began to freeze, sinking into drifts up to your knees. Your exposed skin numbed. Your fingertips and toes throbbed with pain. You trembled and your teeth chattered. Your throat dried with the cold. The wind sliced through your clothes, cracked your lips, forced your eyes to squint until they watered. You heard your own steps crunch through the melting snow, now slippery beneath you. And as the temperature dropped, everything turned dangerous. You wondered how much more your body could take.

The snow changed one brushstroke at a time, shifting from a perfect postcard scene into patches of dirty ice that spread across the roads and eventually turned into potholes. Each winter forced you to learn how to walk all over again. Between the cold, the snow, and the wind, you learned resilience.

Every year you went through the same cycle. The first snowfall, the second, the third, until you grew accustomed to it. And each time you fell in love with the snow the way you did that very first day and hated it just as fiercely the first time it froze your fingers. With the years, your relationship with winter became a toxic one, a love and not-so-much-love affair where every cold season left you waiting for spring.

And somewhere in the city the story repeats. Newcomers see snow for the first time and marvel at things the rest of us have long taken for granted. That is how the Divine reminds us that the smallest things are the ones that truly make us happy.

CHAPTER 27

THE LOVE THAT DISTANCE COULD NOT ERASE

E very heart needs a place to return to, because a house is nothing but walls until love fills it. Finding again what he valued most, beyond any treasure, became his greatest gift, the miracle that gave meaning to every sacrifice. When he finally held Marusha in his arms, life came back to him like a wave of tenderness. He held her tight so she would know he would never leave her alone again, and she answered in the silent language of love, melting into his embrace. In that moment, time stopped. The wind quieted, the cold disappeared, and loneliness dissolved like morning mist. When his daughters joined the embrace, his world felt complete, three hearts bound forever by love and memory.

That night, love was not a word, it was a presence.

It filled the house with a steady light, with laughter, with tenderness reborn. Her kisses carried all the nostalgia of the distance, all the gratitude of coming home again. He traced her face gently, as if rediscovering the map of his own soul. She smiled, and in her eyes, he found the home he had been searching for all along. They did not need words; their hearts spoke in rhythms only love understands.

He remembered then that love had always been his true home. That night was not about desire, it was about return, a celebration of everything that endures when time and distance fail. Nine months later life gifted them a third daughter, and with her came the perfect circle of joy, three daughters, three reasons to believe that love, when it is true, survives every distance.

With the years, the girls' laughter blended with the song of sunrise, and the house filled with small stories: bare feet running down the hallway, little voices inventing songs, hugs that cured any sadness. That house, once silent, became a refuge where every corner breathed love. And although routine settled back in, it was never the same, every gesture, every glance, reminded them of the fragility of life and the strength of beginning again.

Sometimes, in the early evening, he stepped out

into the yard and looked toward the horizon. He was no longer searching for what he had lost, but for what he had found: a family that was both his story and his destiny. Marusha would step out after him, rest her head on his shoulder, and together, in silence, they thanked heaven for bringing them back to the same place where everything had begun, a homemade of love, memory, and forgiveness.

And as the sun hid behind the mountains, he thought of everything still left to live. He knew new trials would come, new paths too, but also new laughter and new dawns. Because if love lived in their hearts, there would always be a future, always a way home. That night, under a sky glowing with stars, he understood that life, in the end, is only that, a round trip back to love.

CHAPTER 28
COQUITO AND NOSTALGIA

There is nothing like being far from the land where you were born to make nostalgia wake up inside you. The gray winter weather only sharpened his longing for his beautiful Borinquen. It arrived without warning, like a whisper from the past slipping between memories. It did not hurt completely, yet it never stopped hurting. It was the smell of Abuela's coffee, the taste of fresh orange juice, the echo of an old song on the radio, and the memory of someone who was no longer here.

When he finally saved enough to buy his own house, the first thing he thought about was filling it with little pieces of Puerto Rico. It did not matter if the walls were cold or if snow covered the street in winter, inside he wanted the warmth of the Caribbean. He hung a flag in the entryway, a reminder of who he was and where he came from. In the kitchen he placed a wooden pilón, even if he did not use it much. On the walls he hung paintings of jíbaros playing the cuatro, tropical fruits, and island landscapes so that every glance felt like a trip back home.

His house became a refuge, a corner where nostalgia softened, because every object, every scent, every detail reminded him that even far away, Puerto Rico lived inside him. He painted the rooms in tropical colors, mixing oranges, reds, yellows, and greens until the house felt like an island breeze. Beautiful photographs of loved ones framed the walls, and with those bright colors there was always salsa music flowing through the speakers. The old speaker thumped like a heartbeat, filling every corner and easing the weight of longing. The living room became his dance floor, his steps a secret conversation with his homeland.

And so, with walls painted in sun and sea, and salsa playing like a personal anthem, his home became an altar of memory, a place where exile did not hurt so much, because every note, every color, every object reminded him that he had never stopped being Boricua.

During Christmas he played aguinaldos and songs from his homeland that transported him back to his youth, back to Tía Carmen's house, where coquito was the undisputed king of the celebration.Titi Carmen measured the coconut milk with the calm of someone who guarded ancient secrets, her apron carrying the scent of cinnamon and sweet memories. On a long table, jars and spoons were arranged like a small map where every ingredient had its own name, cloves, vanilla, a pinch of salt. Beside her, with quiet mischief, Tío Pepe did what he did best during the holidays, challenge her without saying a word. He pulled out a bottle of cañita rum wrapped in onion paper, set it gently on the counter, and smiled like a magician revealing his favorite trick.

The aunt who always knew every recipe moved through the kitchen like a conductor. Her fingers, stained from peeling plantains, measured coconut milk, cinnamon, and vanilla as if telling stories, a pinch of memory here, a sprinkle of laughter there. The cousins gathered around the table like eager apprentices, watching the mixture foam into a tiny cloud as the sweet aroma rose and blended with the Christmas music, turning into an embrace.

Meanwhile, Tío Pepe added his special touch in a

jar on the side, stirring carefully while winking at the cousins. "If you want competition, here it is," he said in his deep voice, offering a little spoonful. The first taste of cañita hit like someone had mixed sunshine and fire in a glass. Lula's eyes widened like two lanterns unsure whether to clap or run. Joshua jumped dramatically, coughed three times, and declared, "This could wake up a dead man." Javi, trying to look brave, swallowed his sip with a face that silently begged his grandmother for forgiveness. Their reactions sparked a chorus of laughter, exaggerated faces, playful complaints, and the certainty that this little spoonful had changed the geography of flavor. The second taste was a clash of worlds: the house recipe, soft and familiar, meeting the warm burn of rum that carried hints of old wood and seaside stories. The young ones saw more than flavors, they witnessed a dance of tradition, a memory each person defended in their own way.

The duel continued through storytelling. Tío Pepe recalled the days he sailed as a young man and learned to measure rum "with a sailor's eye," while Titi Carmen answered with tales from her youth, adding a song to every spoonful. Each story poured into the kitchen like another ingredient, laughter, tender scolding, and advice that slipped in without permission. The cousins became the judges, knowing the real verdict would be how the drink stirred their nostalgia.

When the bottles were filled and the trembling labels read "Coquito de Titi Carmen," a quiet pause followed for the first shared cup. Titi Carmen served her cold coquito in small glasses, and Tío Pepe added a single drop of his cañita to one glass, like signing a pact. Lula closed her eyes as she tasted it, and for a moment the kitchen became a beach: salt on the skin, aguinaldos in the background, cousins laughing. The flavor closed the circle, coconut, cinnamon, sweetness, and memory. The rum did not override the recipe, it deepened it, leaving a whisper of the ocean in the drink.

In the end, no one truly won. The competition faded into long conversations and improvised songs. Tío Pepe and Titi Carmen clinked glasses and teased each other lovingly. What remained was a sweet certainty: in that kitchen, traditions were renegotiated every year, and the mix, whether pure coquito or coquito with rum, stitched memories together. A little was saved under the fridge, out of superstition or affection, and they toasted with the left hand for luck and for the promise the small glass carried: return, remember, reunite. The young ones left with bottles labeled like talismans that smelled of cinnamon and sea, carrying a secret warmth in their chests, learning that homeland fits in a single sip, especially when shared.

He drifted out of those memories and back into reality. The noise of the kitchen, the laughter of the young ones, and the clinking of spoons brought him to the present. The beauty of Spanish words filled the house, seeping into the walls and floor, giving the home a sense of tradition. Outside, the cold bit the skin and snow covered the streets, but inside, the entire Caribbean came alive. Colorful lights hung from the walls, aguinaldos played, and arroz con gandules and pasteles simmered on the stove because, "this is how Christmas is done in Puerto Rico."

During the holidays nostalgia becomes uncontrollable. You develop a new appreciation for the songs you once ignored. You miss things, the barrio, the cousins, baseball games, three on three at the old court, Sundays at the beach. You crave coquito, pasteles, arroz con gandules, and pernil. Where in the world do you find **turrón Alicante**? You go searching desperately for a store that sells Hispanic products. You overbuy sweets of every kind, even if you will not eat them. New Year comes and you miss walking through your barrio plaza hugging and kissing everyone you met along the way.

And Three Kings Day? Forget it. You will not find where to celebrate it, because in your new country it does not exist. The day after Christmas, Santa packs up and the party is over.

Memories are soaked in the flavors and sounds of the past, and where nostalgia lives, melancholy is never far. It is a hurricane of emotions that tries to pull you into its center. The winds of melancholy can cut the heart, can shake you with sadness. When your mind clouds gray, it does not matter if the sun is shining through the window. You surround yourself with photos and close your eyes so that, through the images in your mind, you can hear every sound again. That is how we keep a spiritual bond with what is far away. You want to stretch out your hands and touch everything, but distance will not let you. It is a sad process. It is a roller coaster, emotions rising and falling, laughter and tears, but in the end, it makes you stronger.

And there he was, in a city he did not belong to, trying to belong, surrounded by people he did not know, continuing with his life. Missing everything from his past, forgetting that not everything had been perfect. Deep down he had to admit that many things in the past had not been what they should have been. He should have felt complete with all he had achieved since leaving, yet his homeland kept calling him. He loved her with all her imperfections.

The bright cushions and soft blankets, the curtains

hanging from his window, they dressed his house in warmth. He hung plants in the kitchen that, together with the ingredients for soups and stews, perfumed the air with the scent of Abuela's home. And among the photographs, the snow, and the cold, a feeling of absence awoke inside him, the longing for something that had always brought him happiness, a simple cup of coffee.

CHAPTER 29
ISLAND IN A CUP

"My loves..." he tells his daughters, holding the warm cup between his hands, "if you only knew what a good café colao really means. It's not like the coffee you buy out there on any corner, no... this one has soul."

They say Puerto Rican pride is not shouted, it's served hot, in a small cup, with an aroma made of history. Because in our land, even the homeland gets strained like coffee. Every morning begins with that ancient ritual, café colao. The boiling water wakes not only the body but the memory. In every cloth strainer hide the stories of our grandparents, the crowing rooster, and the songs still alive in the old radio on the kitchen counter.

The first sip always tastes like more than coffee. It

tastes like who we were and who we still are, even when the world changes and the years rush by. That dark, strong flavor, with a sweetness you never forget, carries something of character and something of hope. It is the same mixture that shapes the soul of this island, proud, stubborn, and generous.

While the coffee bubbles, the flag rests on the wall, watching the sunrise. It seems aware of everything, a silent guardian of our everyday history.

The flag and the coffee share an old pact: one waves, the other steams, but both announce the same truth, that there is still fire left in us, that the heart continues beating with the flavor of warm island soil.

Café colao carries the honesty of the countryside and the nobility of simple people. And when its steam rises, it greets the flag waving from the balcony, as if saying, "We are still here." Because being Boricua is not measured by distance, or by passport, or by language.

It is measured by the tremble in your heart when the coffee boils and the flag moves in the wind.

In every house in the barrio there were two things that never failed: a pot of coffee on the stove, and the flag hanging proudly. Abuela always said coffee could fix the world.

If someone was sad or worn down, she didn't ask what happened. "Sit down, mijo. Take a little sip." And the soul understood the message long before the brain did.

Pride is served hot, unhurried, with steady hands, the same way life itself is served on our island that smells of coffee and eternity. And as long as there is café colao and a flag that refuses to surrender, Puerto Rico will keep straining itself into the soul of anyone who remembers.

Our flag is not just fabric, it is heart, memory, and promise. It was born as a symbol of rebellion, in times when waving it was forbidden, a whisper of homeland in the middle of an imposed silence. There was a time when seeing it hanging from a window was almost an act of bravery. But there was always someone in the barrio, stubborn and proud, who hung it quietly, saying without words, "Nobody gives up here."

Now we wear it on shirts, hats, jackets, tattoos... and even if it looks like fashion, it is old love.

When you are far from home and the first winter hits, what saves you from sadness? A little cup of café colao by the window and that flag watching over you with its solitary star.

In cold lands, the flag becomes a coat. In the distance, coffee becomes an embrace. It does not matter if we are in another country, another continent, or another life, the island always travels with us.

The old man paused, blew gently over the foam of his cup, and smiled.

"One day, when I am gone, you will do the same. You will drink a little **café colao** while holding a flag from our homeland... and I will be there too, sitting right beside you, in every single sip."

CHAPTER 30
GIFTS FROM THE DIVINE

As he looked through old photographs, he smiled. Those pictures of his girls drew out joyful memories the way the pages of a beloved childhood storybook return to life in your hands. Happy memories are like sunlight poured straight into the soul, bringing back the kind of happiness you once took for granted in your youth. The older you get, the more those small moments of joy take on a deeper meaning. You savor quiet moments, and you learn to truly appreciate the people you love. Happiness is like a soda, sweet and bubbly and fleeting, and you must enjoy it before it loses its fizz. Luckily, life gives you many refills. Second chances to fix the moments where you once fell short.

He traced each photo with gentle circles of his fingertips. Every picture awakened and played again on the reel of his memory. He stopped at the first one. He remembered the first time he saw her face, how her tiny features glowed with an inner light, and how her little fingers wrapped tightly around his pinky. It moved him to the core. It was as if she were asking him to protect her, and he promised that he would, for as long as he lived, even if it cost him his own life. The more she grew, the more he loved her. He watched her learn to walk, to run on tiptoes, to play with her dolls, to bubble out her first words. That baby was his. The purest feeling, he had ever known took hold of him. Shaken to his core, he knew he would do anything in the world for her. He would be her hero, her guardian, the one who held her close and kept her safe. He would be her dad.

Then came the second baby, with rosy cheeks and wide eyes. She was so delicate he was afraid to hold her at first, afraid he might break that little porcelain doll. Her arrival felt like life had opened a brand-new window in his heart. Her tiny hands repeated the sacredness of the first time, but like a melody played anew. Her older sister looked at her with wonder, and in her eyes bloomed the mystery of shared blood. In that moment he understood that love does not divide, it multiplies, and that every child brings a new light into a family. This little one seemed sent from heaven, and though at first, she cried as if the divine were far away, she soon felt safe in her parents' earthly arms. She was the smallest bundle of joy, and you could not wait to share her with the world.

The third baby girl arrived with a smile that filled him with a light he never knew existed. Her birth felt like life smiling back at them once more, with tenderness multiplied yet again. There was no longer the anxiety of a first child nor the surprise of the second, but a mature joy, calm and steady, like a river widening without losing its current. Her closed eyes seemed to guard the mystery of all the words not yet spoken, and her brief cry filled the house with a brand-new music. Her two sisters, still small themselves, looked at her as if they had discovered a treasure. And in that instant, he knew that the heart never tires of loving; it always finds room to bloom once more. Such a great miracle in such a tiny being. There were no words to describe what he felt each time he looked at her. He hoped that someday she would understand how much of her father's heart belonged entirely to her.

Daughters are gifts from the Divine, and divine in their own right. He would forever be grateful that his daughters had chosen him to be their father. There was nothing he would not do to keep them safe from harm, even while knowing he could not protect them forever. But one thing was certain: he would always be there, each time they stumbled, ready to help them rise again, and to stand beside them as they reached for the stars.

CHAPTER 31
THE JOURNEY

He had to move forward because there was no other choice. The years passed and he walked. When the road was cold, he walked, and winter taught him how to stay warm on the inside. When the road was rocky, he walked, and the sharp stones forced him to become lighter. When it rained, he walked, because rain was a blessing on the hottest days. When the sun burned, he walked, because sweat reminds us, we are alive, that we love, that we dance. When life drove thorns into him, he walked, even if his feet bled, because he knew that stopping hurt even more. You must walk, because the road does not care what you are made of. The road wants only one thing, that you travel it, and that you learn as you move forward.

On the road he met new friends. Never like the friends of childhood. Childhood friends feel as if they were placed there by the Divine. New friends are like the image on an instant camera, blurry at first, then sharpening slowly until you can finally see them for who they are.

On the road he met others who were not such good friends, lonely souls looking for company or asking favors. Some were temperamental, petty, dishonest, pessimistic, rude, resentful, selfish, insensitive, even paranoid. In the vineyard of new friendships there was a little of everything.

On the road he learned to feel what others feel, because empathy is like a firefighter who runs into a burning building just to save your life, feeling your fear and your pain in the process.

On the road he met despair, loneliness, melancholy, nostalgia, pain, anguish, love, peace, compassion, and many other emotions. Life had become his greatest teacher.

He learned that every fall has its own language. That sometimes you do not get up to keep going, but to understand why you stumbled. Pain, when you look at it directly, stops being an enemy and becomes a guide. And he understood that life, more than a journey toward a destination, is a constant conversation with oneself.

There were nights when the silence was so heavy it felt like it had a body of its own. But it was in those nights that he discovered the soul also breathes in the dark. He learned to listen to himself without fear, to hold his own heart when no one else could.

Like the trees, he had to learn to lose his leaves to be reborn. There were winters in which he felt dry, empty, without color. But he understood that even the bare tree keeps life hidden in its roots, waiting for the moment to bloom again. He learned that stillness is also part of growing, and that quiet moments are sometimes only the prelude to renewal.

And when his own spring finally arrived, he blossomed without realizing it. It was not an explosion, but a gentle awakening, a kind gesture, a new laughter, a more patient gaze. He discovered that you do not need all the answers, it is enough to keep growing toward the light, just as trees do after the storm.

Little by little, the road stopped being only dirt and stones. It became a mirror. Each step returned a different version of himself, freer, more aware, less tied to the past. Walking, he learned that life is not about running from pain, but about walking with it until it grows tired and dissolves.

Sometimes he found flowers growing in the most

improbable places, right where the earth seemed barren. Then he understood that hope is exactly that, a flower that does not ask about the season, a flower brave enough to bloom even in the middle of winter.

He also discovered that there are people who walk with you only for part of the journey, and that is alright. Not everyone reaches the end, but everyone leaves something behind, a word, a glance, a footprint that teaches you to look at the horizon in a new way.

In the end, he understood that the destination is not at the end of the road, but in every step. And that if there is love, memory, and gratitude, there will always be a reason to keep walking. Because life, like the heart, is not measured by what you accumulate, but by what you are able to give as you walk.

CHAPTER 32
THE ROAD THAT BROUGHT HIM HOME

He woke from that dream and his eyes drifted toward the horizon. The sun's rays struck him hard, almost blinding, as if urging him to look deeper. Ahead lay a long, ascending stretch of road leading to the entrance of the town that had once cradled his childhood. And when he finally reached the top, the sky opened like a curtain, and he looked down at the breathtaking vastness of the mountains. The view stole his breath.

The mountains lined the horizon, touching the blue ceiling of the sky. Palms swayed by the coast, and the sea, calm as a sleeping giant, framed the shoreline where his memories lived. The sky glowed a soft, misty blue, and in that moment he knew. He had come home. Somehow, despite worries, distance, and the heavy changes of a lifetime, he had returned to the place that first said his name.

Returning to the land where you were born is like revisiting an old love. You want to impress it, the way you would before a first date. But at first, it can disappoint you, looking a little faded, less magical than in memory. You need time to rediscover the small details, the quirks, the imperfections, the hidden beauty that slowly bring the love back. The feeling reveals itself the way an old Polaroid develops, soft and slow, until the full picture appears before your eyes. It enters you gently, settles into your soul, and you fall in love all over again.

An old love never truly dies. It becomes a song buried beneath the noise of life. All it takes is one note, one scent, one laugh, one melody on the radio to wake it again. The heart, even when it pretends to be steady, remembers how to tremble. An old love is scar and flower both. It hurt, it healed, and still, it blooms inside you. It becomes a companion, a whisper that says, "I was here, I am still here." In time you learn that life is not about letting everything go, but about learning to walk with the echoes of what shaped you.

Your homeland is the greatest love of all. It is the house of your spirit. Nature itself is family. When you are born with boricua blood, you carry the palms, the rivers, the mountains, and the coquí's nightly lullaby inside your veins. There is a magic in living in this paradise, a quiet fire that you never lose, no matter where you go.

Forty years had passed since he last lived in his beloved Puerto Rico. Life had slipped away between work, distance, family, and silence. His island, once an old love, had become a new one, familiar yet transformed. And with each passing day he understood the truth: people change, places change, barrios change. You cannot hold on to the illusions of the past. The buildings are not the same, the streets are not the same, the people are not the same. Time moves forward, and the ones who move with it survive. Life pushes you toward the new, though adaptation comes slowly. If he wanted to belong again, he had to evolve too.

Home is a feeling of serenity in the soul. Everything else, comfort, routine, familiarity, is optional. Changes may challenge you, but in the end, you will be alright. The island would love him, but he could not forget that he had to love it back.

The emotions he had buried deep for decades rose like a sudden tide. He remembered the scent of warm bread, of guava and lilies, of sea salt in the breeze. He remembered sunburned streets, the quiet after a storm, puddles of mud, and the drowsy sweetness of a siesta after lunch. He remembered the sand climbing between his toes and the foam kissing his ankles. He remembered the nights full of stars, when time stopped and the coquí began a serenade that lasted until dawn. Being in Puerto Rico again felt like finding a long-lost friend, and it was tender, overwhelming, beautiful.

He walked the same streets, passed the same houses, greeted the same people, yet nothing was exactly as he had left it. Perhaps it was foolish to believe it would be. His friends welcomed him with tight embraces and laughter, catching up as if no time had passed at all. There is something magical about hugging an old friend, because beyond the embrace, you are holding years of memories, late-night conversations, street-corner jokes, improvised fiestas. But little by little he saw the truth: the void he left had long been filled, and only the scars remained. He was no longer part of their rhythm. Something felt misplaced, slightly off, like a song played in the wrong key. Time had reshaped them all. Age had carved its marks. And though he expected it, the realization still hurt.

Old age had once seemed far away, a horizon you never quite reach. But step by step, it had caught up with them. Youth had been left behind like a forgotten bag at a bus stop. Some complained that life had traded their strength for wisdom. They spoke of choices they regretted, dreams they never chased. Often, they closed their eyes quietly, imagining themselves young again.

The barrio of his childhood no longer hummed with the same energy. Silence sat where shouts once echoed. Abandoned cars stood where children once played barefoot. The neighbors' voices had faded. No one told stories on the corners anymore. Houses painted with laughter now wore colors of forgetfulness. Don Toño's store was gone. The music from the bar near the plaza had died. Even the stray dogs seemed to have disappeared. The new residents walked differently. They did not know the names of those who came before them, while the barrio watched them in silence.

Still, something always remains in some corner, in some quiet doorway. Doña Yiya, sitting in her old rocking chair, still remembered him, waving into the air as if greeting the ghosts of the past. Yes, the barrio had changed, but its soul lingered in the walls that had heard laughter and in the memories of the elders who refused to forget.

The elders of the barrio are the pillars that hold together the social and cultural fabric of the community. They carry history in their wrinkles and tradition in their voices. They guide the young the way lighthouses guide ships. They are proof that resilience can be gentle, that wisdom can be generous. Listening to them is a privilege, one that grounds you. They are the heartbeat of the community, a reminder of what truly matters.

Of course, the barrio had changed physically and generationally. The music was different now. The thing that shook him the most was the "**voceteo**," a heart of vibrating speakers mounted on four wheels. It was vibrant, loud, and chaotic, a cultural phenomenon both fascinating and frustrating. But tranquilo Bobby tranquilo, the youth also have the right to their own language, their own beat.

His return home marked a new beginning. It felt like life handing him a second chance. And the greatest irony of all was this: in returning to his past, he discovered that the one who had changed the most, was him.

CHAPTER 33

THE THREE "BAD" KINGS

What never changes, although it sometimes unites Puerto Ricans and other times divides us, are three sacred things, religion, politics, and sports. Those three topics have sparked more arguments, hugs, rivalries, and reconciliations than anything else in the island's history. In every home there is an altar, a flag, and a television ready for the Sunday game. And deep down, all of it has to do with faith, faith in God, faith in the political parties, and faith that this year the Capitanes, the Indios, or the Leones will finally win.

In Puerto Rico, religion is not just a Sunday ritual, it is part of daily life. Some people go to the ten o'clock Mass, with the smell of incense and the soft voices of the choir, and others get ready for the Pentecostal service, where the hallelujahs rise higher than the speakers of a music car. Both places have their charm. In the Catholic church, the priest greets everyone as if he had known them forever, and the parishioners respond with solemnity, or with sleepiness if the homily goes on too long. In the Pentecostal temple, the joy spills over, hands rise, drums echo, and even the neighbors who stayed home end up hearing the preaching through the window. In one place you pray calmly, in the other you sing with fire. But in the end, the faith of the people is the same, and that blend of prayers, promises, and panderetas is what keeps the Boricua soul alive.

If religion moves the soul, politics moves the tongue. In Puerto Rico, politics is inherited like a last name. You are born knowing the color of your family, and during election season the front yard becomes a headquarters. Speakers shake the neighborhood, balconies get painted, and even the roosters seem to pick a side. Political debates happen in the barbershop, in the bakery line, or at the domino table. No one escapes. Grandpa swears that everything was better before, and the grandson argues that real change is finally coming. Every four years they promise heaven, a train to the west, and the end of blackouts. The only guarantees are traffic on election day and a Monday hangover. And still, we vote with hope, like someone playing the lottery, knowing it probably will not hit, but dreaming that maybe this time it will.

Sports are our great national therapy. When Puerto Rico plays, there is no PNP, no PPD, no independentista, we are all Boricuas with our hearts in our hands. Baseball, basketball, and boxing have given us heroes who feel like family. The streets would empty when Tito Trinidad stepped into the ring or when the Puerto Rican Dream Team walked onto the court. And on every corner, there is an expert claiming that if he were the coach, Puerto Rico would have already won the World Classic. They give us pride, identity, and a reason to celebrate.

In our homeland, sports were always more than a game. They moved crowds as if they were a sacred ritual, they dominated hearts and divided feelings with the same force that a storm splits the sky. We saw sports unite towns, yes, but they also broke friendships and created rivalries that went far beyond entertainment. At times they served as a convenient hiding place, a curtain that concealed the country's real problems while people celebrated a victory or mourned a loss. And while many gave their souls to a team, those in power learned to use that passion to push agendas, justify expenses, and distract the people from what truly mattered. In this way, without noticing it, that third king, sports, ruled our emotions with a mixture of pride, fervor, and a silent power that still runs through the stadiums like an old rumor that no one wants to speak of, yet everyone has felt.

In the end, those three topics, religion, politics, and sports, are the mirror of who we are, passionate, stubborn, and full of dreams. But they also explain, in their own way, why bipartisanship has taken us to where we are, in debt, divided, and waiting for the next miracle. We have spent decades caught between broken promises and recycled speeches, as if the island were a game that never ends. While the politicians argue about who is to blame, the people keep working, praying, and dreaming of a better future. And even as the debt grows, Boricuas never lose faith, because here, even when the numbers refuse to add up, there is always hope that the next game, the next election, or the next prayer might change the story.

CHAPTER 34
GRANDMA'S HOUSE

There is nothing sadder than walking past the old house that watched you grow. Your grandmother's house. The place of memories, long talks, and gentle advice. Everything looks so much smaller than it did when you were a child, and you wonder how everyone ever fit inside those four little walls.

There it stood, worn down, miserable, and abandoned. What once were beautiful windows were now enormous holes where the wind entered and left whenever it pleased. The front door hung from worn walls and hinges covered in rust, tilted at an angle that made it look like a scarecrow. The grass around it had grown long and wild. If there had ever been a path, it had vanished. Water stains ran over the peeling paint like scars on skin.

A strange feeling forced him to stop and step inside. He fought through the tall grass until he reached the door, which fell off its hinges the moment he touched it. Once inside, he stumbled over pieces of the ceiling that had fallen onto the entrance. Around him lay the artifacts of a life once lived and long abandoned, mattresses, dolls, photographs. The house felt strangely silent, and the only thing he could hear was his own breathing and the soft crunch beneath his feet with each step. It felt as if a sleeping spirit had awakened at his presence, shy now and wanting to stay hidden. The smell of dampness from a house abandoned for too long filled his nose. Cobwebs clung to every corner. The house that once welcomed everyone now seemed ashamed to be seen, dark, old, dirty, and worn. It was as if it had become aware of itself, of the history still echoing inside its walls.

He could not help thinking that somewhere deep within this sad house, mixed with its pain, there were images of happiness. He felt as if the spirit of the house was asleep within the walls, resting in the memories of its early years, when it was young, full of laughter, music, and color. Now this poor house could only listen as the wind whistled through, carrying the laughter of children who were not its own.

As he touched the cold walls to keep his balance on the rubble, every inch released memories of his childhood. The house had not felt the touch of a human hand in years. Cobwebs brushed his face as he walked deeper inside. There was a silent desolation in this house that had once been full of joyful sounds. He stopped, the house stopped, and time stopped with them. He closed his eyes while running his hand along the wall, and he could see everything as it once had been. The decorations, the curtains, the checkered tablecloth on the dining table, the bedroom doors, his grandmother's keepsakes, the photos on the walls, and the smell of her cooking. He wanted to touch the surfaces his grandmother had touched, hoping that some part of her still lived within this house.

He felt as if the house remembered him. It seemed to cry, longing for the last time it saw them play and heard their laughter. It was dying slowly, missing the warmth of a family, and had grown tired of fighting. It had learned to love its loneliness and to become one with the spiders. It could no longer resist the elements or the passing of years. This small, proud, powerful house, once loved so deeply, was now a crumbling shell like old bread. A house once cherished, then abandoned.

He gathered his strength and walked toward the small kitchen, now crowded and full of dust. The cabinets were faded. The countertops were missing, probably stolen long ago. Thieves had taken anything of value. A thick gray layer of dust covered the wood and the floor. What remained of the sink was stacked with old plates. Insects and plants had claimed the kitchen for themselves. Plants pushed through cracks in the walls, and a small chicken's nest rested inside one of the drawers. He gave one last look toward the back of the house, where sunlight touched the dark remnants of the room where he slept as a boy. It was dim and gloomy, with a couple of frames hanging crooked on the walls. He felt powerless and deeply sad. He tried to close his eyes and focus on something beautiful, pure, sacred, anything that could distract him from the heaviness of the moment. He remembered lying down to listen to music, reading comic books, and sharing jokes with one of his cousins. He looked around the small room and remembered how few belongings he had back then, yet he had lacked nothing. On the contrary, in that room he had everything he ever needed. He could not think of a single moment in which he had been missing anything.

He stepped out into the yard and touched the door-frame as if saying goodbye to an old friend. "Do not worry, old house. One must die to be reborn. A new family will come to your door, they will make you new again, and you will be young once more, much younger than I am." He ran his hand across the frame one last time, gave it two gentle taps, and whispered, "Thank you."

What once was a garden was now a field of tall grass. He looked toward the tree where an old swing hung motionless and silent. He wondered how long it had stayed there, alone in the wind, waiting, always waiting for laughter and play to return. Once it had been a throne for princes and princesses, their favorite place in the whole world, but now it was nothing more than a rotting piece of wood hanging from a rope, gathering dust in a deserted yard.

That abandoned house was a story of return in progress. Perhaps there was a time when he wished it would fall apart completely, but not anymore. For some reason, despite the decay, it remained standing. It had been battered by storms, yet there it was, refusing to fall. And so, instead of seeing its cracks as flaws, he saw its face telling the world, "I am still here, and I will rise again." Within its abandonment, it had learned to sing with the wind and lean toward the sunlight.

It was a goodbye, and they both knew it. That old house would live forever in his memory.

CHAPTER 35

THE SILENCE OF THE ROCKING CHAIR

I t is impossible to walk through the little house that once belonged to his grandmother without feeling his soul fill with her voice. He stood in silence, looking at the old house. He had walked through it slowly, step by step, like someone crossing the ruins of a church, and now he watched it from the yard. On the balcony there was an emptiness that had its own shape, the shape of Abuela's rocking chair. The creak of that chair had once been the music of dreaming wood, the gentle rhythm that marked the hour of the afternoon. He could swear the patio still breathed her memory, a faint breeze lifting the dust as if her skirt brushed the floor again and her soft laughter hid among the flowerpots.

He closed his eyes, and the murmur of her prayers returned, a river of words that seemed to know his fears and his silences. Her life, so simple, had been a perfect clock, dawns awakened before the sun, hands that began the day, a patience that healed, a tenderness that never asked for applause. She had a gift for lifting what weariness knocked down, for fixing the world with a single touch. With her small habits she raised them all, children and grandchildren alike, through the strength of example. She taught them to save bread, to listen first, to speak softly when someone else's soul was hurting. She taught them that faith also cooks slowly, like sofrito, and that love does not shout, it whispers.

At night her rocking chair went back and forth, and with each movement the house breathed easy. He learned his own name from her lips, and courage from the look in her eyes that never judged. When he closes his eyes he still sees her folding sheets, serving food like someone who serves hope. Her tenderness, never rushed, carried them through the years and shaped them into who they became.

Abuela was like the mango tree in the yard, steady, sweet, and generous even in her shade. She never needed a compass or a clock, because time for her was marked by the roosters at dawn and the position of the sun throughout the day. Her colao coffee perfumed the home before the sun peeked through the flamboyanes. She wore flowered house dresses and soft sandals that announced her steps, and she was the keeper of the family's secrets. With one hand she served you rice and beans, and with the other she blessed you against the evil eye. On her lips there was always a saying, a prayer, or a story explaining why the world was the way it was.

Abuela knew how to heal with malagueta leaves, whispered prayers, and breaths offered to the wind. If your stomach hurt she made you an infusion with anise and rue. If your heart hurt she wrapped you in her arms and said, "This too will pass, my love."

She was a queen without a crown. On her table there was never a shortage of arroz con gandules, pernil, and a trembling piece of tembleque. Daughters and granddaughters learned from her how to cook and how to wait, because life, she said, cooks slowly, like sofrito.

Abuela had a gift, she made time stop. You could spend hours listening to her stories about Hurricane San Felipe, the fiestas patronales, or the impossible loves that were never told completely. In her eyes lived an entire country, the countryside, the beaches, the mountains, and the nostalgia.

And when she sat on the balcony in her rocking chair, looking toward the ocean with her thoughts far away, you understood that it was she who held their world together with her patience, her faith, and her unconditional love.

The mothers of today are the daughters of those strong grandmothers who learned to do much with little. In every Puerto Rican mother, there is a piece of her own mother, that woman who taught her to rise early, to cook with love, to be strong even when the soul aches.

The grandmothers shaped our mothers and aunts through example, not speeches. They taught them that a home is not held up by walls alone, but by love, work, and respect. They taught them that crying is not weakness, but a way to clean the soul. That is why our mothers keep going, even when exhaustion becomes a companion.

From them they inherited the habit of serving others first, of keeping old photos in a shoebox, of naming every plant, and of thanking God for the little or the much. And yes, they also inherited the legendary aim with the chancleta, able to correct any mischief from a distance with almost magical precision.

In every gesture of our mothers, when they rub our forehead, when they prepare the rice, or when they defend us without thinking twice, there is the voice of a grandmother whispering from the past, "This is how it is done, mija."

This is why, when we look at our mothers, we also see our grandmothers. They are the invisible roots that support them, the echo that guides their decisions, the tenderness living in their eyes. Because grandmothers never die. They become breeze, song, and memory. They live in prayers, in old photographs, in the laughter that rises from the kitchen. They are the soul of the home, the heart of the past, and the root of everything we become.

A soft breeze touched his forehead. It was no coincidence, and he knew it instantly. Love does not disappear, it changes shape, it becomes warm air, light on the floor, silence that keeps you company. He stood in front of the house and understood that she was still there, alive in the quiet of the rocking chair, in the stubborn smell of coffee that never fully leaves, in the murmur of a prayer that was never finished. He knew too that as long as he remembered her, as long as he repeated her gestures and her kindness with others, his grandmother would continue breathing in him. The yard grew still again, and in that silence, he learned once more how to say thank you.

Today, Abuela is no longer here, but her voice still

echoes in the yard where the plantain trees and ferns grow. Her presence still lingers whenever the breeze smells like freshly brewed café colao or when someone proudly says, "That is how my grandmother used to do it."

CHAPTER 36

UNDER THE PALM TREES SLEEPS BLUSON

He could not leave that place without saying goodbye to a very special soul, the truest companion of his childhood: Blusón, a sato with a heart larger than the mountains. By now he must be in dog heaven, that place where the souls of those who knew how to love go to rest. He never needed papers or pedigree, because his lineage was written in the hot earth and in the dust of the streets where he grew up.

The satos of the barrio were part of daily life, like the corner store or the song of the coquí at dusk. They ran behind bicycles, joined the games in the street, and waited for children outside the school gates. They always seemed to know exactly who needed company that day, as if instinct whispered the answer.

His name was Blusón because they found him inside a small blue box. He was cinnamon-colored, with pointed ears and the noblest eyes in the world. He followed him everywhere, to spin tops in the street, to pick mangos, and even to church on Sundays, where he waited quietly under the bench until the service was over. He did not know manners, but he knew love. If someone yelled at his master, Blusón stepped between them, chest held high, defending what was his.

Toñito had a sato called Manchas, who always smelled like wet earth. Manchas was mischievous, an expert at stealing bread from the bakery and sneaking into baseball games. Doña Carmen had Luna, a white sata with black spots who slept on the balcony and guarded the grandchildren as if they were her own.

The satos were family, even if no one said it out loud. They shared arroz con salchichas, soft bread from breakfast, and even a sip of soda from the can. They slept under chairs, beside the chicken coop, or curled up beside a sick child, as if they understood human pain better than anyone. Sometimes they disappeared for days, and an emptiness settled in the heart, like the absence of a brother. But they always came back, tail tucked, eyes saying, "Here I am," and you knew the house was not complete without them.

In those days there were no fancy veterinarians or

elegant collars. All they needed was a bit of rice and the affection of the entire neighborhood. Satitos did not require much to be happy, only freedom, love, and a place where someone would be waiting for them.

The day Blusón died, the whole neighborhood felt different, as if the sun had risen more slowly. Friends gathered without saying a word, eyes shining, chests tight. They made him a small but solemn procession with flowers taken from Doña Pola's Garden and a cross made from palm branches.

They carried him in an old fruit crate and walked together to the sand dunes near the edge of the beach. The wind blew hard, and the sea seemed to understand their silence. They buried him under the palms, in the same spot where he had chased waves so many afternoons. Someone prayed a Padre Nuestro, someone else placed a small stone on his grave, and before leaving, Toñito left an old baseball next to the cross. They said goodbye without crying, but with a knot in their throats. They felt they had lost more than a dog, they had buried a friend, a piece of their childhood.

Today, when we walk through the streets of our island and see a sato running free across the fields, we feel as if we are seeing Blusón, or Manchas, or Luna. They look at us, wag their tails, and keep going. And you know that somehow those dogs never truly left, they are still running through the patios of memory, guarding our childhood, barking at the ghosts of time.

And ever since, every time the wind blows through the palms, we swear we hear a distant bark coming from the sea. Perhaps it is Blusón, reminding us that loyalty and love are never buried, they simply turn into memory.

CHAPTER 37

THE SCENT OF GUAVA

S ometimes joy and sadness mix, and sometimes I think they are meant to. Memories, both the sweet and the painful ones, are photographs stored in the soul.

He loves returning to his old neighborhood to walk through its streets and rebuild his happiest moments. Memories often rise through a fragrance. The moment he reaches the entrance of the barrio, a familiar scent opens the album of warm and moving memories and takes over the air.

The unmistakable smell of the sea drifts through the neighborhood, the salt in the air, the scent of the beach and of rain that makes you feel as if you are living in an endless summer. The sea breeze is like a soft towel offering its warmth. These scents carry him back to La

Poza del Obispo, to el peñón, to the curve beach, to the lighthouse, to the pier, and to the hiding places in the hills.

There are scents of the coast and there are scents of the countryside. On the coast, the air is ruled by seafood, fried fish, alcapurrias and bacalaítos. In the countryside, the world smells of damp earth, freshly cut grass, wildflowers, wood, straw and lechón roasting. But there is one scent that enters the deepest part of his being and plays a gentle lullaby in his heart. That scent is guava.

The smell of guava that lingered in the air was sweet, strong and penetrating, like a memory that refuses to leave. It arrived with the morning breeze, mixing with the roosters crowing and the aroma of café colao drifting from the kitchen. For us, the kids in the neighborhood, it was almost a signal. We ran to the yard to look for ripe guavas, to climb the tree or pick them from the ground, biting into the fruit still warm from the sun.

The grandmothers bought guavas from the boys who walked through the streets selling them in large tin cans. With those guavas, they made homemade jelly and **casquitos de guayaba**, little candies made from the fruit's skin. The process was simple but filled with love. First, they boiled the guavas until soft, then mashed them and cooked them again with sugar until they became a thick, sweet, glowing jelly. The casquitos were made by boiling the skins with sugar, then letting them dry until they turned chewy and full of flavor. Nothing tasted like that jelly they spread on bread or crackers, sweet, tart and carrying a grandmother's love in every bite.

That scent was not just fruit, it was the aroma of childhood, of the countryside, of a simple life that taught us to find joy in the most natural things. The smell of guava brings back childhood and the people you loved, grandmothers, cheerful aunts, cousins and neighborhood friends who are no longer here. It makes you smile or makes your eyes fill with tears. When you catch the scent of guava, it feels as if one of them has returned and is standing right beside you.

CHAPTER 38
THE LITTLE TOWN SQUARE

Things were simpler fifty years ago because life itself was simpler. We did not have video games or computers to take up our time. There were no social networks, and we were not worried about someone stealing our identity. Everyone in the neighborhood knew us by name and shared everything, from a little cup of sugar to a hammer. We were a family for better or for worse, and we knew each other well. Even with the occasional fight, we were loyal, affectionate, and protective of one another. Back then, fun came from playing sports, swimming, fishing, or simply running wild through the neighborhood. Life in the barrio gave us a huge playground wrapped in nature to explore. Now it seems as if we have become prisoners inside our own homes.

Walking through the barrio, he was surprised by the number of metal bars covering the windows. Theft had begun feeding addictions and had become an addiction of its own.

Inside every abandoned house, he could see a kind of emotional indifference. Each of those empty buildings had its own story. The bar that once filled the night with music and a pool table. The corner store that had a little bit of everything. The small shop that was once someone's dream come true. The fritters made with so much love, the gift of someone's talent to the community. The cheerful characters and the small business owners who supported their families by working day and night. But now only memories remain, good ones, joyful ones, and sometimes painful ones.

Memories are like small photographs, chosen to create a little album of our best moments. In the barrio, the songs of the birds, the percussion of the waves, the fragrance of passionfruit, the smell of salt in the air and of frituras, the smile of the sun, the sound of a carpenter's hammer fixing something, and the noise of children playing during recess were the cause of our happiness. These memories arrive like a beloved relative we have not seen in a long time, who suddenly appears in the doorway and fills the room with a smile.

We save the good memories in case the bad ones try to appear. The painful memories are books with chapters, deep and terrible, and for that reason we prefer to leave them on the shelf to gather dust.

From the little plaza in the barrio, you could once see the beauty of community in motion. We loved it so much that we called it "la placita." It was the heart of the neighborhood. On a sun-warmed bench, parents found joy in watching the children play while the elders played dominoes. The teenagers danced salsa, skated around the benches, or experienced their first love. But now it spends most of its time lonely, faded, and forgotten. The new generation has no idea of the placita's golden years.

That space witnessed laughter that still seems to float among the trees. Sundays smelled of empanadillas and freshly brewed coffee, the air filled with the sound of domino tiles hitting the table and with loud, unrestrained laughter. Every afternoon had its own color, its own music. It was the place where ages, voices, and dreams mixed, where no one was alone because life was shared without hurry.

In the placita one learned without teachers. There, you discovered that happiness did not need much, only a worn-out ball, an old radio playing salsa, and the feeling of belonging to something that beat larger than yourself. The community was the soul, and the placita was its body. Everything happened there, the advice, the gossip, the crushes, the scoldings, the improvised birthdays. It was the school of the heart.

But time, with its quiet steps, began taking away the elders who filled it with stories. The benches lost the voices that once warmed them. The domino games were left unfinished. The children grew up, and the young people left in search of a future that no longer fit in the barrio. Little by little, the placita remained alone, like an album with no new pages, watching the days pass.

Now the paint is peeling off in pieces, and Don Ismael's store, the one with the jukebox that was the heart of the place, is gone. Yet if you sit there long enough, you can still hear something. It is as if the wind carries old echoes, a laugh, a song, the whistle of a passing bicycle. Memory never dies completely, it only falls asleep, waiting for someone to wake it up.

Sometimes a child runs across the plaza again, and for a moment the place comes back to life. The trees seem to straighten themselves, the air fills with that childhood scent you never forget. Maybe not all is lost. Maybe the placita, like the best memories, only needs someone to believe in it again in order to be reborn.

Because in the end, neighborhoods do not die, they only change their voice. And as long as someone remembers, the placita will remain alive in some corner of the soul, waiting for a new generation to return its music, its laughter, and its life.

Perhaps the elders who still remain can teach the young about the golden years of the placita, when the air was filled with music and the soul of the neighborhood beat strong. El Gran Combo played there, Andy Montañez, Chivirico, Tommy Olivencia, La Patrulla 15, Yolanda Rivera, the lady of salsa, and so many others who made our nights vibrate. Few know that in that small corner some of the most joyful fiestas patronales in the region were celebrated, climbing the greased pole, sack races, boxing matches, and small pageants where the entire neighborhood gathered to cheer.

The placita was more than a place, it was a celebration of who we were. As ours as arroz con gandules and pasteles at Christmas, as alive as the laughter that filled the afternoons. It was where generations, voices, and dreams met. It was a little piece of heaven in the dust, a refuge where life tasted like community and hope.

Today, however, it seems asleep. Its empty benches keep the echo of old songs, and its ground, covered with dry leaves, still remembers the steps of those who danced there until dawn. The placita grows old in silence, like a faded photograph that refuses to disappear, waiting for someone to look at it again with the eyes of the heart.

CHAPTER 39

THE SOUNDS OF EL BARRIO

It was a Friday afternoon in the barrio and the sun was slipping behind the dome of the Catholic church. The breeze carried the smell of fried food and gasoline when suddenly, in the distance, a roar rose strong enough to make the ground tremble. The windows of the nearby houses rattled, yet no one ran outside. They knew it was not an earthquake, it was Benito, arriving with his *voceteo*.

The corillo leaned out to look. Benito's blue Suzuki turned the corner with its doors open, like the wings of a metal bird. The lights flashed to the beat of the music, and every hit of the bass thumped in your chest, like having a second heartbeat. That car was proof that you do not need luxury to impress anyone. The Suzuki with its *voceteo* was the voice of boricua ingenuity, taking the little you have and turning it into a lot. The engine sounded humble, but the speakers roared like dragons. Everyone in the barrio knew who had arrived and, even though the car was old, it dressed itself in youth with every note. It was like an old man with a young spirit, worn on the outside but roaring with strength just to remind everyone he was still here.

Benito arrived with his beastly sound. People murmured, the elders complained, and the young ones smiled with that quiet complicity. The doñas crossed themselves, the kids danced trying to imitate him, and the whole barrio became the audience of that rolling concert. Yes, he was a *vocetero*, but he was also a declaration of life, a shout against routine, an electric poem saying, "I am young, I am free, and no matter how hard you try to quiet me, I will sound louder than you."

That afternoon, the barrio burned with energy. The reggaetón made the ground vibrate as if the earth itself had a heart. The girls were not listening to the music, they were feeling it in their skin, their laughter, their hips. The vibration of the bass pulled them in. And while the older folks heard nothing but noise, to the youth it was a sweet melody that lived only in their world.

The bass pounded like an invisible hammer and eardrums, fragile as they were, trembled like candles in a storm. The music, which had once caressed, now felt like a blade, a burning needle piercing the ears and leaving a hot echo in the head. It was a strange pain, a mix of pleasure and punishment, as if the joy of the moment demanded a price with every vibration. Some laughed, not understanding the complexity of it all, and they looked at the other elders who stood terrified. Their ears begged for calm, but the bass never stopped.

In that moment it became clear that music, when it spills over, can hurt just as much as bad memories. And look at that, and we were the ones saying the *placita* was dead. Not at all, it just needs some company on Friday afternoons. Maybe those moments will inspire the raguetoneros to give it a fresh coat of paint.

CHAPTER 40
STRONG AS CEIBA TREES

María arrived with an infernal mood, she blew, she killed, she cut and destroyed with a fury we had never seen before. I had never heard such a savage scream or witnessed such a dense torrent. It was obvious that María came angry, determined to cause enough damage that we would never forget her. Never had the clouds gathered like that, heavy, dense, so dark it seemed the sky was about to collapse. Her passing felt like an eternity, and she did not tear only our roofs, she tore our souls and our hearts with the hand of trauma.

The night before, the air already smelled strange, as if the wind carried a warning. Some people filled bottles with water, others prayed, and Don Manuel stood by the window watching how the trees leaned as if bracing for the blow. When María arrived, she came with a noise like a hundred trains roaring over the house. The zinc roof lifted with every gust and Don Manuel, arms outstretched, tried to hold on to the impossible. Water seeped through every crack and the floor turned into a river. Outside, nothing existed except darkness and flying branches. Inside, there were only a handful of hearts beating fast, huddled together, hoping the house would not split in two.

María arrived with wings of fury, with a scream of wind that ripped mountains and tore the green from the island by its roots. She did not ask permission, she swept away roofs like pages from a book, drowned the nights in the darkest blackness and left the coquí singing alone, suffocated in the silence of the rain. The water rose like a river overflowing with tears, houses were left naked, and on every corner a cry blended with the roar of the hurricane.

The wind was so wild and the rain so fierce that nothing felt safe. Anything that was not tied down went flying like a projectile. Under every door and through the shutters, water forced its way in, trying to invade our home. The house trembled and made strange sounds, just like the pets who cried and whimpered, terrified by the howl of the storm. María's fury shattered windows as if they were made of paper. Her winds came to interrupt every bit of peace. The trees collapsed and fell on the power lines. We were left in darkness, terrified, worried about the families who lived in the little houses near the river. We lit candles and flashlights. The rain filled the rivers until they burst from their banks, the dams threatened to break, and the chocolate-colored water carried away things we held dear. María was furious and nothing could stand in the way of her anger. There was no man or beast and much less any structure that could stop her. She was a wounded monster that wanted to hurt us. All we could do was pray for that nightmare to pass quickly, because it is in these savage moments that true believers are born.

At dawn, the silence hurt more than the noise. The mountain that had always been green now stood bare, as if the entire forest had been burned to the ground. The power lines hung like dead snakes and the town looked like another planet, without light, without signals, without color. But after the roar came the unity. The neighbors came out, one lent a generator, someone else brought coffee in a big pot. Together they improvised a kitchen in front of the basketball court. Neighboring hands lifted debris, pots were shared among strangers, candles glowed like rebellious stars in a sky that seemed to have gone dark. María hurt us, but she also reminded us that we are fragile like branches and strong like the ceiba that grows back. The hurricane had knocked down trees, roofs and towers, but it could not knock down our habit of taking care of one another.

What had José done to make her take it out on us like that? María arrived like an enraged wife and threw every single plate in the kitchen at us. Nothing was left whole or intact or pristine. With one torn scream she made sure everyone heard her, and that no one could ever forget her.

And from that day on, we learned that nature remembers too. That the wind has memory, that the rain knows how to cry, and that clouds can hold grudges. But we also learned to rise, to sweep up the pieces and to give thanks for every new day in which the sky chooses to give us a breath. Because even though María marked us, we are still here, alive, stubborn and boricua, resisting like the palm tree that bends but does not break, because we are strong like the ceiba trees.

CHAPTER 41

IN FRONT OF THE YELLOW GATE

They say that "good fences make good neighbors," but in the barrio, a neighbor can become your dearest family, and sometimes even the person you fall in love with.

Mariela lived in the yellow house on the corner, with the windows always open and the smell of sofrito drifting out every afternoon. Jorge, on the other hand, lived across from the basketball court, quiet, with a shy smile, always willing to carry the grocery bags of the older ladies in the neighborhood.

They had known each other their whole lives, though they had barely exchanged more than a "good morning." But the hurricane changed everyone's routines. That morning, while the barrio remained without power, Jorge showed up with a pot of freshly brewed café colao and offered some to Mariela.

She looked at him surprised, accepted the cup and smiled.

"I didn't know you could make such good coffee."

He shrugged, cheeks turning red.

"I learned thanks to all these blackouts."

From that day on, every afternoon they met at the yellow gate. She rested her elbows on the sun-faded bars while he, on the other side, held the coffee thermos like a treasure. The warm metal of the gate kept the heat from their hands, and when the wind blew, it felt as if the iron itself breathed with them. They shared pan sobao and talked about everything: how the barrio had changed over the years, the music that still spilled into the streets, the dreams that never go out even when the island trembles.

Little by little, the barrio regained electricity. But between them, a different kind of light was born, a brightness that did not depend on cables or generators. The yellow gate remained there as witness to that simple love, born from silence and the smell of café colao.

The neighbors began to whisper that Jorge passed by the yellow house every day, that Mariela smiled more than before. And one day, with no mystery at all, they were seen walking to the plaza hand in hand, as if it had always been that way. In the barrio, love does not hide. It blooms during blackouts, on old sidewalks, and under the knowing gaze of neighbors who secretly celebrate every new story.

That is how life works in the barrio. From any little corner a surprise can appear, and next to a yellow gate, love can begin.

CHAPTER 42

FROM ANY NET A MOUSE MIGHT EMERGE

In the barrio everyone respected Don Ernesto. He was the model neighbor, dressed in a suit every Sunday for church, always with the lawn trimmed and the car spotless. No one doubted his correctness, and many held him up as the example of what a good man should be.

One afternoon, Doña Carmen sent her grandson to fetch a ball that had fallen into Don Ernesto's yard. The boy jumped the fence and, instead of finding the ball, came across a small cage hidden behind the shed. Inside, a few squeaking mice were waiting, kept there to feed his boa, an enormous snake he was secretly raising.

The news spread through the barrio faster than credit at a corner store. "But look at that! Don Ernesto

with a snake in his backyard, who would've thought?"
The ladies whispered through their laughter, and the
kids started calling him Don Ernesto the snake
charmer.

The next morning, Don Ernesto stepped outside,
red-faced but composed, and said calmly,

"Well neighbors, you can see now that from any
little corner a mouse can appear, even in mine."

And while Don Ernesto walked around the barrio
looking like a martyr, another worried neighbor was
praying to God that he wouldn't release the snake into
the hills, afraid that one day it might turn into an inva-
sive plague of reticulated pythons.

When he lingers on the memory of his old neighbors, he feels warmth. The loving laugh of Doña Elisa.
The comforting words of Doña Rafaela. The tender
voice of Doña Gogi. The good humor of Doña Titi and
Don Tito's jokes. The good cooking of Doña Adela and
Doña Rosa. In those memories he finds comfort and
refuge. He cannot remember a single moment when
neighbors kept their doors closed. He walked into their
homes as if they were his own, just like "Juan por su
casa", and only now realizes how impertinent he might
have been.

He believes the happiness of others' lives in how we
treat them, and ours in how they treat us. Because in

that barrio the good neighbors who knew you by name or by a nickname also had the luck of knowing your heart. They shone like the sun and suffered when we suffered. They prayed with you when empathy was needed, cried with you, did not know indifference, and loved without fences or the poison of judgment. Whenever a storm or disaster arrived, whether from nature, crisis, or illness, those neighbors brought out the best in themselves and rushed to help. There is no chicken soup as good as the one a neighbor makes for you. There is no one better to help patch a roof or board up windows before a storm.

Neighbors are like pieces of a puzzle we slowly fit together until they form a beautiful landscape. The barrio is a river where we all swim, and the neighbors are the water, filled with the smiles of new joys and the celebration of old memories and wisdom.

It is true, neighbors, like our island, are truly something else.

CHAPTER 43
OLD AGE AND SOLITUDE

He had reached the age where pain, wisdom, and the search for joy all meet. He did not feel old, but he was tired from the battles he had fought. He lived quietly now, though his laughter could still fill a room. His steps had slowed, and the little hair he had left looked almost angelic. There was a gentle intelligence in his appearance. His face belonged to someone who had lived, suffered, and loved deeply. Perhaps it was the kind of wisdom that only arrives with the years and that is paid for with tears of every kind. He had learned that each day is a gift from the Divine, and that old age is a privilege. His smile and his eyes revealed a man who had discovered a new appreciation for life.

Old age, like one step after the other, slow but

steady, had arrived inevitably. It had taken some of the obvious senses, but it awakened something he had ignored during the excitement of youth, a new calling toward what we call the spiritual. It was hard to imagine what he must have looked like when he was young. He had become a grandfather to all the younger people around him. He felt love for everyone, and his mission now was to share the wisdom he had acquired through experience, the kind that comes only with age and maturity, the kind learned through pain and memories that rise directly from the heart.

He had dodged death long enough to earn his wrinkles. To his grandchildren he was a hero. Now nothing entertained him more than old stories, old songs, a good cup of red wine, and a little glass of pineapple-coconut ice cream. His only hurry was to leave something behind, a small legacy for those who would remain after him. People now called him "sir," and treated him as an old man. But inside he still carried a young soul who loved to play with his collection of baseball cards and toy cars. That inner boy would always stay playful and silly.

He had that look in his eyes, the look of a life well lived, one where love had sat in the front row through the hard times and the good ones. His voice was still strong, but his tone had softened. His wrinkled hands spoke of tenderness, and though gentle, they had once been capable of moving mountains. Trembling now, yet still precise when love guided them. The lines around his eyes were stories of laughter, warm smiles, and affection. His forehead held the worries that remained. His shoulders were the favorite place to rest, like a pillow made of feathers. His arms were a safety net, an emotional harbor where the weather was always perfect, and the sun always shone. His chest was a refuge for every kind of storm.

What he could not escape was the loneliness that had become his only trustworthy friend. Nothing had touched it, not romantic adventures, not familiar faces at the bar, not the friends he made online. Loneliness was not merely the absence of company. It was a black hole that grew stronger with every passing day. His trips to the town café were simply to pretend, even for a moment, that he was not so alone.

Sometimes he felt so lonely he could hear the beating of his own heart. It was as if everyone else's journey in life had drifted far away from his. Loneliness squeezed his heart with such pressure that it became a constant ache. But it was his cross to carry. Over time, he learned how to ease the pain. He began to see his loneliness as a reminder that nothing in life is perfect. He learned to fly alone. He learned to rise to new heights and see things he had never seen before. His room became like the sky to a bird, an endless canvas.

There are cycles in life that are painful, but they are the same ones that let you rise again like a phoenix.

Old age is not so bad when you can look back and feel proud of the road you walked, and even more so when you can still walk through the streets of your barrio and remember. Because, ¡¡**To Remember Is To Live**!!

CHAPTER 44

PUERTO RICAN CULTURAL GLOSSARY

Acerolas: Small, bright red tropical cherries rich in vitamin C, often used in juices or jams in Puerto Rico.

Agüeybaná: The legendary Taíno cacique (chief) of Borikén who welcomed the Spanish upon their arrival in the early 1500s.

Aguinaldos: Traditional Puerto Rican Christmas songs, often sung in parrandas with guitars, güiros, and maracas.

Bacalaitos: Crispy codfish fritters sold at beach kiosks; salty, thin, and absolutely addictive.

Barrio: A neighborhood or small community; often refers to one's local roots or place of belonging.

Bomba: One of Puerto Rico's oldest musical genres, of African origin; a lively dialogue between drummers and dancers.

Bonito y Barato: (Pretty and cheap). B and B (Bonito y Barato) was a department store in Arecibo.

Borincano: A person from Borinquen (the Indigenous Taíno name for Puerto Rico); synonymous with Puerto Rican pride.

Borinquen: The original Taíno name of Puerto Rico, meaning 'Land of the Brave Lord.'

Café colao: Traditional Puerto Rican brewed coffee made by hand through a cloth strainer called a colador.

Caldero: A heavy aluminum or cast-iron cooking pot with thick walls and a tight-fitting lid, used in almost every Puerto Rican kitchen.

Cambalache: A historic sugar mill district in Arecibo

Cantalisio: The iconic advertising character from Corona beer commercials. When you invite a friend to have a beer you call him Cantalisio.

Cafres: Refers to someone who is rude, uncultured, tacky, loud, or lacking manners.

Casa alcaldía: The town hall or municipal building, often located in the plaza.

Casquitos de Guayaga: A traditional Puerto Rican sweet made from the peel of the guava fruit, gently boiled with sugar until soft, glossy, and candied. Often served on their own or with a slice of cheese as a simple, beloved dessert.

Ceti (seh-tee): Tiny transparent post-larval fish caught at river mouths, a local delicacy eaten fried or in fritters.

Ceiba trees: Giant, sacred trees found across Puerto Rico; symbol of wisdom and endurance in folklore.

Chancletas: Flip-flops or sandals; also famous as the 'weapon' of Puerto Rican mothers used for discipline.

Chicharrón: Fried pork skin, crunchy and flavorful; often sold with yuca or tostones.

Chinchorro fishing: A traditional fishing method using nets near the shore, often done by families or groups. It is also used to describe a small food stand.

Chinchorrear: To go hopping from one roadside bar or food stand to another, eating, drinking, and socializing all day.

Cholchas: Blankets or comforters, often sold by door-to-door vendors in Puerto Rico.

Cocotazo: A playful or disciplinary knock on the head with the knuckles; a mother's way of saying 'Pay attention!'

Come Gofio: Literally 'gofio eater'; used teasingly for someone naïve, gullible, or at times used to describe a pretentious or stuck-up person who *forgets where they came from.*

Coquí: The tiny frog that sings 'co-quí' all night; an emblem of Puerto Rican identity and nostalgia.

El Campo: The countryside; rural Puerto Rico, known for its peaceful pace and traditional customs.

El Cielo: El Cielo Dept Store, in De Diego Avenue in Arecibo. It appears in a list of shops of the past in Puerto Rico, a store from earlier decades. Literally means The Heavens.

El Corillo: A close group of friends or crew; your inner circle.

El Fuerte: The site originally housed Fuerte San Miguel, a Spanish colonial fortification built to protect Arecibo from attacks and pirates. In 1881 the fort ruins were transformed into a promenade known as the "Paseo de Damas" (Ladies' Walk) or "Paseo de Damas / El Fuerte". It is now commonly called Paseo Víctor Rojas, named after a local hero (fisherman/rescuer) from Arecibo.

El grito de Lares: The 1868 uprising against Spanish rule; considered Puerto Rico's cry for independence.

El pueblo: The town center or community itself; also symbolizes 'the people.'

El show de las 12: A classic Puerto Rican midday television variety show that ran for decades, featuring music and comedy.

Empanadas: Fried or baked turnovers filled with meat, cheese, or seafood; in Puerto Rico often called pastelillos.

Flamboyán tree: A bright red-flowered tree that blooms in summer; a symbol of beauty and nostalgia.

Fulanito: 'So-and-so' or 'what's-his-name'; used when you forget or don't want to say someone's name.

Frituras: A variety of Puerto Rican fried snacks typically made from doughs, batters, or seasoned fillings like seafood, meat, or vegetables. Common examples include alcapurrias, bacalaítos, empanadillas, and sorullitos.

Garabato: A garabato is a crooked branch or stick with a natural hook.

Gofio: A sweet, powdery snack made from toasted cornmeal or wheat flour mixed with sugar.

Come gofio: Literally 'gofio eater'; used teasingly for someone naïve, gullible, or at times used to describe a pompous or arrogant person.

Guagua: A bus or large passenger van; also used for public transportation across the island.

Guaraguao: A red-tailed hawk common in Puerto Rico; sometimes used symbolically for vigilance or pride.

Icaco: Is a tropical coastal fruit tree common throughout the Caribbean, especially in Puerto Rico, where it grows naturally near beaches and mangroves.

Jalea Casera: Homemade fruit jelly, often made by simmering ripe fruit (like guava) with sugar until thick and spreadable. In Puerto Rican homes, it is traditionally enjoyed on bread or crackers.

Jíbaro: The traditional Puerto Rican mountain farmer; symbol of simplicity, wisdom, and authentic island identity.

Jurutungo: A faraway, hard-to-reach place; 'He lives way out in Jurutungo' means 'in the middle of nowhere.'

La Borinqueña: The national anthem of Puerto Rico, celebrating the island's beauty and heritage.

La Comay: A famous Puerto Rican TV gossip puppet known for scandal and satire.

La Gloria: Literally "The Glory". Also, a Puerto Rican department and shoe stores founded around 1940.

La "Jamona": or "solterona": a single, older woman, usually one who has never married or doesn't have a steady partner *"past the age people expect her to.*

La loma del tamarindo: A popular Puerto Rican song written by Wiso Santiago whose lyrics reflect nostalgia for childhood, work, honesty or a symbolic place often used to describe a small rural area.

La monga: Puerto Rican slang for a cold or flu; 'Tengo la monga' means 'I've got the sniffles.'

La poza del Obispo: A natural beach pool in Arecibo, famous for its waves and beauty.

La Prera: A program that provided financial aid, food, and jobs to poor Puerto Rican families.

Majarete: A sweet, creamy dessert made from cornmeal, coconut milk, and cinnamon.

Malanga: A root vegetable similar to taro, boiled or fried; a staple in traditional cooking.

Mofongo: Mofongo: A traditional Puerto Rican dish made from fried green plantains mashed with garlic, salt, broth, and crunchy pork rinds, shaped into a mound and often served with meat, seafood, or savory sauces.

Pan sobao: Soft, slightly sweet Puerto Rican bread with a chewy texture.

Parranda: A musical Christmas celebration, similar to a *caroling serenade*, but louder, happier, and filled with *boricua sabor*.

Pasteles: A pastel is a savory dish made from a grated root-vegetable dough (masa) filled with meat, wrapped in banana leaves, and boiled

Pastelillos: Fried turnovers similar to empanadas; stuffed with meat, cheese, or pizza filling.

Pedro Navaja: A fictional character from Rubén Blades' salsa classic, symbolizing street life and poetic justice.

Penepés: Supporters of the pro-statehood political party, Partido Nuevo Progresista (PNP).

Piraguas: Shaved-ice cones with flavored syrup, sold from colorful roadside carts.

Plena: A traditional Afro-Puerto Rican musical style that tells stories of the people through rhythm and song.

Pleneros: Traditional Puerto Rican musicians who play *plena*, a folk genre known as "el periódico cantao." Pleneros use hand-held frame drums called *panderos* and sing call-and-response lyrics that tell stories about community life, celebrations, and social events.

Pomarrosas: Is a tropical fruit tree also known in English as the Malay rose apple or mountain apple.

Populares: Supporters of the Partido Popular Democrático (PPD), generally pro-commonwealth.

Pitirre: A small, fearless gray bird that defends its nest even against hawks; a symbol of Puerto Rican courage.

Pa' allá fuera: Literally 'over there outside'; refers to the U.S. mainland where many Puerto Ricans migrate.

Otra cosa: Literally 'another thing,' but used to mean 'something special' or 'amazing.'

Otra vez fría: Literally 'cold again,' said when something doesn't work out the way you hoped.

Puertorro: Slang for Puerto Rican; often used affectionately or with pride.

Puñeta: A strong Puerto Rican exclamation expressing

frustration, surprise, or excitement; similar to 'Damn!' or 'Wow!'

Public car: Informal shared taxis or minibuses that operate along fixed routes, often faster and cheaper than buses.

Que se los lleve el diablo: Literally 'may the devil take them'; an exasperated phrase used when talking about corrupt politicians or bad luck. Can translate into "the hell with them".

Quenepas: Small green fruits with a thin shell and sweet pulp; eaten by cracking them open and sucking the seed.

Quincalleros: Traveling merchants or peddlers who sell trinkets, tools, or small household goods.

Raguetón (Reggaetón): A musical genre blending reggae, hip-hop, and Latin rhythms; born in Puerto Rico.

Recao: A leafy herb used in sofrito; similar to cilantro but with a stronger flavor.

Sandunga / Sierva sandunguera: Sandunga means lively rhythm or swagger; sierva sandunguera playfully refers to a spirited, joyful church woman.

Sofrito: A blended mix of garlic, onions, peppers, recao, and herbs, forming the base of Puerto Rican cooking.

Satos: A mixed-breed or stray dog.

Tapón: Traffic jam or heavy congestion

Tostones: Twice-fried slices of green plantain, crispy on the outside and tender inside. A classic Puerto Rican staple served with salt, garlic mojo, or as a side to almost any dish.

Turrón de Alicante: Spanish almond nougat, traditionally eaten at Christmas.

Juan por su casa: Expression meaning 'acting like you own the place' or 'walking around carelessly.'

The Flying Nun: Reference to the 1960s TV show starring Sally Field, popular in Puerto Rico; used jokingly for someone overly pious or naive.

The Three Kings: The Reyes Magos; central figures of Puerto Rican Christmas traditions celebrated on January 6.

Que se los lleve el diablo: Literally 'may the devil take them'; an exasperated phrase used when talking about corrupt politicians or bad luck. Can translate into "the hell with them".

Víspera de San Juan Bautista: The eve of the Feast of Saint John the Baptist, celebrated on the night of June 23 in Puerto Rico with music, beach gatherings, and the traditional ritual of falling backward into the water at midnight for good luck.

Voceteo: The Puerto Rican car-sound culture of

blasting music through huge speakers; a mix of pride, rebellion, and rhythm.

Vaporú: Puerto Rican nickname for Vicks VapoRub, the cure-all ointment used for colds, fevers, and heartbreak.

ACKNOWLEDGMENTS

Acknowledgments

To all those who, with their memory and affection, helped me rebuild the fragments of this story. To those who shared their laughter, their anecdotes, and those everyday details that now bloom in these pages. To my family, for their constant love and infinite patience. To my friends, for keeping alive the bonds that time could never erase. And to my homeland, for continuing to inspire every word written from the heart.

A very special thank you to Professor Kevin Fuentes Rosas, for his valuable contribution with the chapter *"La Sandunguera."* To all those who once told me, "tell the story, so it won't be forgotten," thank you, because without you this book would not exist.

With affection and gratitude,
SFernando Carmona

ABOUT THE AUTHOR

SFernando Carmona is a thinker and storyteller whose passion for memory and culture shapes every word he writes. Born and raised in Arecibo, Puerto Rico, his voice carries the rhythms, humor, and tenderness of the island that formed his spirit.

Through his work, he seeks to preserve the beauty of everyday life, the laughter of family, the wisdom of elders, and the nostalgia that unites generations.

Recordar es Vivir is his tribute to homeland, to family, and to the art of remembering, a celebration of the stories that remain alive within us and of the cultural roots that keep them burning. When he writes, Carmona not only tells his own story but also honors those who came before and inspires those who will follow, especially his daughters, to whom this book is lovingly dedicated.